DP
DEMPSEY
PARR

PREMIERSHIP WINNERS

by
Jon Palmer

PREMIERSHIP
WINNERS

First published in Great Britain in 1998 by
Dempsey Parr
13 Whiteladies Road
Clifton
Bristol BS8 1PB

ISBN: 1-84084-206-7

Produced for Dempsey Parr by Prima Creative Services

Editorial director Roger Kean
Managing editor Steve Faragher (Content E.D.B.)

Design by Maryanne Booth (Content E.D.B)
Repro by Prima Creative Services

Printed and bound in Italy

Acknowledgements
The publisher would like to thank Tim Smith (Content E.D.B) and Steve Bradley for
their invaluable help in the production of this book.

Picture Acknowledgements
The publisher would like to thank Allsport for their help and the kind permission to
reproduce the photographs
used in this book.

Contents

Introduction

two seasons in one

For many, including one bookmaker, there were two 1997-98 Premiership seasons. The first was won by Manchester United before Christmas... but the New Year saw Arsenal rampant...

Coming into 1998, the Red Devils were going to win the title, the FA Cup and the Champions League. One bookie even paid out... but Arsenal stirred as the Reds dipped, and "Season 1997-98 – Two" began.

At the end of "Season One", Barnsley were heading straight back down. But the Tykes' post-Christmas form placed several "bigger names" on the slippery slope.

By the start of "Season Two", mid-table was a bear-pit with Newcastle, Spurs and Everton occupying slots usually held by an energised Coventry City, a secure Southampton and still-in-London Wimbledon. Villa, Leicester, Liverpool and Wednesday all began "Season One" in dismal form only to be vying for Europe by the time New Year rolled around.

Indeed, the scrap for European places went to the wire.

A third season was added by FIFA; the fight for World Cup places added spice (and Spice Girls). Skill levels were also increased by the influx of first-string foreign imports. And no one illustrated how English football could mix and match to everybody's advantage better than the eventual champions, Arsenal.

Bergkamp, Anelka, Wreh and Overmars produced finishes of awesome class. Ray Parlour was a new player in the magnificent midfield of Petit and Vieira. From a team of also-rans at the start of "Season One", Arsenal finished as champions with two games left to play, the FA Cup shining brightly, and the Champions League beckoning next term.

PRE-SEASON ODDS 1997/98

MAN UTD	11/10
NEWCASTLE	7/2
ARSENAL	9/2
LIVERPOOL	9/2
CHELSEA	12/1
VILLA	20/1
BLACKBURN	50/1
EVERTON	50/1
SPURS	50/1
LEEDS	80/1
SHEFF WED	100/1
BOLTON	150/1
WIMBLEDON	150/1
COVENTRY	200/1
LEICESTER	200/1
WEST HAM	200/1
DERBY	250/1
SOUTHAMPTON	250/1
PALACE	350/1
BARNSLEY	500/1

(Odds quoted from research done by *Total Football* magazine)

HOW THE PREMIERSHIP FINISHED IN 1996/97

Man Utd	38	75	(Champions League)	Leeds	38	46	
Newcastle	38	68	(Champions League)	Derby	38	46	
Arsenal	38	68	(UEFA Cup)	Blackburn	38	42	
Liverpool	38	68	(UEFA Cup)	West Ham	38	42	
Villa	38	61	(UEFA Cup)	Everton	38	42	
Chelsea	38	59	(Cup Winners' Cup)	Southampton	38	41	
Sheff Wed	38	57		Coventry	38	41	
Wimbledon	38	56		Sunderland	38	40	(relegated)
Leicester	38	47	(UEFA Cup)	Middlesbrough	38	39	(relegated)
Spurs	38	46		Forest	38	34	(relegated)

NATIONWIDE DIVISION ONE

Bolton	46	98	(promoted)
Barnsley	46	80	(promoted)
Wolves	46	76	
Ipswich	46	74	
Sheff U	46	73	
Palace	46	71	(promoted)

CARLING CHAMPIONS

CARLING CHAMPIONS

Manchester United looked set to repeat the
success of 1997-98 until Arsenal awoke

Welcome to the fight
1997–1998

This season has seen more upsets, dramas and superb play than any other in the brief lifespan of the Premiership. Recapture those memories in full-colour with all the information you need

Team-by-team we look at the runners and riders that made this Premiership season a talking point throughout the world. Foreign imports showed just how much the English had learned while the domestic talent went from better to much, much better...

ARSENAL

Arsène Wenger comes over from Japan to try his luck here and signs half the Monaco team as replacements for the ageing Highbury First team...

8

ASTON VILLA

Stan-the-Man came home and last season's meanest defence bar Arsenal should have been right up there challenging for the championship. What went wrong? **10**

BARNSLEY

"Plucky", "Spirited", "Going straight back down"... all that maybe true but every so often it was still "just like watching Brazil" all over again

12

BLACKBURN ROVERS

Roy Hodgson faces his toughest challenge yet, the English Premiership. He has a record as good as any manager, but does his team have the legs for the league? **14**

BOLTON

The Premiership's premier yo-yo team came bouncing back again ... this time with a team good enough to stay up comfortably. Or so we all thought...

16

CHELSEA

Gullit built England's best cup team, but could they now challenge for the League? And what would happen when Ruud leaves the Bridge? **18**

COVENTRY

Going down this time, surely. Not if new manager Gordon Strachan has anything to do with it. He always demands the proverbial 110% from his players **20**

CRYSTAL PALACE

The Eagles seemed intent on securing survival through some clever dealing in the transfer market, but could they find the players they'd need to stay up? **22**

for the Premiership

DERBY COUNTY

A new stadium and an exciting team playing attacking football brought the promise of a year of consolidation in the Rams' second season back up in the top flight... **24**

EVERTON

Andy Gray is linked with his former club as the Toffeemen seek a new manager over the summer, but Gray is quite happy where he is these days. Kendall it is then... **26**

LEEDS UNITED

Right. That's the defence sorted. Now to buy three midfielders and a new striker. And stick the lad Rodney up front too. See how he likes life at the sharp end **28**

LEICESTER CITY

After coming up via the play-offs a year ago, the Foxes went straight into Europe as Coca-Cola Cup winners. Could they repeat the feat and go further? **30**

LIVERPOOL

4-4-2, 5-3-2, or 3-5-2? Does it really make much difference when the team doesn't even seem to believe it can achieve its glory days of the past 25 years? **32**

MANCHESTER UNITED

The Champions have their eyes on European glory but they were also looking to win the league for the third successive year. Could they both this year? **34**

NEWCASTLE UNITED

Second last time out, second the time before that. Both times to Manchester United. Surely the Magpies could do it this year. Especially with Shearer on form... **36**

SHEFFIELD WEDNESDAY

Wednesday have the worst first half of a season they've seen in quite a while. So out goes David Pleat in comes Ron Atkinson. Can the big man save the day? **38**

SOUTHAMPTON

No Le Tiss, a manager no one outside Division Two has heard of and Southampton look like going down after years of struggle and mediocrity. But... **40**

TOTTENHAM HOTSPUR

New manager Christian Gross hops over from Grasshoppers of Zürich to save Spurs from sliding into trouble... Has anyone got Jürgen's new phone number? **42**

WEST HAM UNITED

Harry Redknapp does some more crafty dealing in the transfer market and comes up smelling of roses once again. But when's Jamie going to London? **44**

WIMBLEDON

Are the Dons going to Dublin? Or will Merton council find them a home? Or neither? Whatever happens, Wimbledon were tipped to do well this year **46**

Arsenal

the gunners

The question was how much Arsène Wenger would tamper with the tightest back four in English football. But when he saw them play, he chose to leave well alone, and Arsenal won the league

It was plain from the start that the likes of Dixon, Winterburn, Bould, Keown and Adams were not the kind of players with which Arsène Wenger usually operated. England's tightest back four was a legacy of George Graham's days at Highbury. Although they had been far and away the most parsimonious defence in English football for a decade, they didn't play the ball out from the back, and they were getting on a bit too.

Wenger had signed Emmanuel Petit and Gilles Grimandi from his former club as possible replacements, but when he saw Graham's defence in action, he saw no reason not to keep it intact. So Petit moved into midfield, where he and Ray Parlour supported the defence from the flanks, while Grimandi

played a bit part on the bench. Meanwhile at the other end, Overmars fitted in well with Wright and Bergkamp and Arsenal began the season looking a good outside bet for the Championship.

Wins against Southampton, Chelsea and West Ham sent the Gunners to the top of the league, but they were rarely capable of reproducing the form that had destroyed Barnsley. Then Petit got himself sent off against Villa and Bergkamp collected enough yellow cards to earn a ban; two vital players would be out through suspension until after the Man United game. Arsenal won that match anyway, but it seemed then that any hopes of the title had slipped away already. So rather than thoughts of the Premiership, the big talking points at this time were the cup

runs and the club's proposed move to Wembley. Having been thwarted by local residents in their plans to expand Highbury, Arsenal FC looked to take over the national stadium as their own ground, though they eventually chose to abandon this idea: "In the interests of English football."

Soon after that matter was resolved, Arsenal began to play like nobody else. The team's incredible consistency in the final run in, when they never tired and never looked like losing, was too rich a vein of form for Manchester United to keep up with. Nicholas Anelka came to prominence and scored some vital goals. When Arsenal beat Manchester United again, the race for the Premiership was well and truly back on.

CLUB FACTS	TRANSFERS IN				TRANSFERS OUT			
Stadium: **Highbury** (0171) 704 4000	Jul '97	**Christopher Wreh**	Monaco	£300k	Mar '98	**Vince Bartram**	Gillingham	free
Capacity: **38,500**	Jun '97	**Alex Manninger**	Casino Graz	undisclosed	Feb '98	**Valur Gislason**	Stromsgodset	undisclosed
Manager: **Arsène Wenger**	Jun '97	**Alberto Mendez**	FC Feucht	undisclosed	Feb '98	**Jehad Muntasser**	Bristol City	free
Club captain: **Tony Adams**	Jun '97	**Marc Overmars**	Ajax	£5m-7m	Oct '97	**Glenn Helder**	NAC Breda	undisclosed
	Jun '97	**Luis Boa Morte**	Sporting Lisbon	£1.75m	Oct '97	**Ian Selley**	Fulham	£500k
Premiership record	Jun '97	**Emmanuel Petit**	Monaco	£3.5m	Sep '97	**Paul Shaw**	Millwall	£250k
1992/93 **10th**	Jun '97	**Gilles Grimandi**	Monaco	£1.5m	Jul '97	**Paul Merson**	Middlesbrough	£4.5m
1993/94 **4th**	May '97	**Matthew Upson**	Luton	£1.5-2m	Jun '97	**Adrian Clarke**	Southend	free
1994/95 **12th**					Jun '97	**Lee Harper**	QPR	£125k
1995/96 **5th**					May '97	**Matthew Rose**	QPR	£0.5m
1996/97 **3rd**								

GAME OF THE SEASON

Saturday 18th April
Arsenal (3) 5 Adams 12, Overmars 17, Bergkamp 19, Petit 54, Wreh 88.
Wimbledon (0) 0
Att: 38,024   Ref: Jones

Arsenal scored three times in the first 18 minutes and Emmanuel Petit bagged his first goal for the club. John Motson called it: "The best football I have seen all season." And that's quite a lot of football. It was the first time Arsenal had beaten Wimbledon in the League at Highbury since 1987 and it could have been double figures.

Tony Adams played the best football of his career this year to lead Arsenal to glory

Aston Villa

the villans

After the performance of the Villa defence last year, the fans expected Collymore and Co to bring them some glory this season. They were to be disappointed

Something obviously went horribly wrong at Villa Park over the summer. When local boy Stan Collymore arrived from Liverpool, there was grand talk. "Hopefully at the end of the season we will have some silverware to show off," said Collymore when he arrived. Even if he hadn't been at his best in recent times, Colly was a quality buy. Surely he would flourish now that he was playing for the team he had supported as a boy. And if the defence stayed as mean as it had been throughout the previous campaign, perhaps Villa would even win the title.

But when the season began, Villa started leaking goals badly as the team got off to its worst ever Premiership start. They couldn't score at the other end either. Collymore wouldn't find the net at Villa Park until the Coventry game in December and it was left to the unsettled Savo Milosevic to lead the attack. With Dwight Yorke as good as guaranteed a First team place whenever he was fit and available, Savo had been expected to leave the club when Collymore signed and he looked certain to go after he fell out with Villa's fans during the match against Blackburn. But the Serb stayed despite interest from Napoli. He scored the winner against Bordeaux and followed that with the only goal of the match at Bolton in the league, a game in which Collymore was sent off after an argument with Andy Todd.

By Christmas, Villa had reached the quarter–finals of the UEFA Cup, but their league form was so poor that their Premiership survival was now in serious jeopardy. The problems in attack were obvious enough, but it was hard to say why the defence wasn't performing. With the exception of Mark Bosnich's injuries and enforced absence during Australia's ill-fated World Cup qualifying campaign, there was little to upset the rhythm. But something was wrong, and Brian Little was eventually replaced as manager by John Gregory.

This proved the fillip the team needed as they slowly clawed their way up the league in the spring. But the fans will be expecting a better performance next year, especially as this campaign ended with Gregory seeking to extend the contracts of key players Bosnich, Charles, Draper and Joachim.

CLUB FACTS

Stadium: **Villa Park** (0121) 327 2299
Capacity: **39,339**
Manager: **Brian Little, John Gregory**
Club captain: **Gareth Southgate**

Premiership record
1992/93 **2nd**
1993/94 **10th**
1994/95 **18th**
1995/96 **4th**
1996/97 **5th**

TRANSFERS IN

Jun '97	**Simon Grayson**	Leicester	£1.35m
May '97	**Stan Collymore**	Liverpool	£7m

TRANSFERS OUT

Mar '98	**Sasa Curcic**	Crystal Palace	£1m
Mar '98	**Steve Claridge**	Wolves	£350k
Dec '97	**Scott Murray**	Bristol City	£150k
Sep '97	**Stuart Brock**	Kidderminster	free
Sep '97	**Matthew George**	Sheffield United	free
Aug '97	**Andy Townsend**	Middlesbrough	£500k
Jul '97	**Gareth Farrelly**	Everton	£700k

GAME OF THE SEASON

Friday 26th December
Aston Villa (1) 4 Draper 38, 68, Collymore 81, 89
Tottenham (0) 1 Calderwood 59
Att: 38,644   Ref: Wilkie

When Villa lost at White Hart Lane in August, it was their fourth defeat on the trot. But when Spurs came to Villa Park, the Holte End sang: "Are you watching Andy Gray?" as Collymore silenced the critical Sky TV pundit with a convincing performance capped off with two late goals to double his tally for the season.

Mark Bosnich gets some stick from the Spurs
fans after his foolish misdemeanours last year

Barnsley

the tykes

Where Oakwell had seen gates of around 7,000 for most of last year, every game this season was a sell out as Barnsley played their first ever season in the top flight in their 110-year history

In hindsight, Barnsley were always doomed to go straight back down to the Nationwide League. But at the start of the season, everyone said they were doomed to finish bottom by a street. In the event though, the Reds put up a good fight and weren't relegated until the very end of the season. One more win and the celebrations of last year would have been repeated.

In truth, it was rarely "just like watching Brazil," as their fans sing, but at times it was, and at least the team stuck to their footballing traditions instead of trying to shut up shop against the big boys and play the percentage game. The Tykes earned some good results this year and last season's free-scoring midfielder Neil

Redfearn immediately proved that he was, as he'd always thought he would be, good enough for the top flight. The captain scored the Tykes' first ever top flight goal on the opening day and then netted the winner at Selhurst Park three days later to put Barnsley eighth – just as rivals Wednesday began their slump into the drop zone.

The Chelsea match was a case of "crash bang wallop!" according Danny Wilson. But when new signings Tinkler and Hristov did the job against Bolton, it ensured that the Tykes would end August in the top half. It couldn't last, of course, Hristov wouldn't score again until the return against Bolton on Boxing Day, by which time some heavy defeats had lifted Barnsley's goals against ratio to over three per game.

The team soon found that the Oakwell faithful were capable of turning on them. Now that Barnsley were up, the fans wanted them to stay there; one season of glory wasn't enough. But some serious thumpings at the hands of the top clubs always made survival look unlikely. Danny Wilson wisely took on Jan Aage Fjortoft when Sheffield United started offloading all their decent strikers, but in the end, even his goals weren't enough.

But there were moments. Like Ward's goal against his old club Derby and Bosancic's debut strike against Blackburn. And this summer, at least one Barnsley player will get the chance to prove that he is as good as Brazil; Eric Tinkler should play for South Africa in France.

CLUB FACTS

Stadium: **Oakwell (01226) 211211**
Capacity: **18,806**
Manager: **Danny Wilson**
Club Captain: **Neil Redfearn**

Premiership record
1992/93 **13th (Div 1)**
1993/94 **18th (Div 1)**
1994/95 **6th (Div 1)**
1995/96 **10th (Div 1)**
1996/97 **2nd (Div 1)**

TRANSFERS IN

Jan '98	**Jan-Aage Fjortoft**	Sheffield United	£800k
Nov '97	**Peter Marksted**	Vasteras SK	£250k
Sep '97	**Ashley Ward**	Derby	£1.3m
Aug '97	**Darren Barnard**	Bristol City	£750k
July '97	**Ales Krizan**	Maribor Branik	£500k
Jun '97	**Eric Tinkler**	Cagliari	£650k
Jun '97	**Georgi Hristov**	Partisan Belgrade	£1.5m
Jun '97	**Lars Leese**	Bayer Leverkusen	£300k
Jun '97	**Tony Bullock**	Leek	undisclosed

TRANSFERS OUT

Mar '98	**Steve Davis**	Oxford	£75k
Sep '97	**Paul Wilkinson**	Millwall	£150k

GAME OF THE SEASON

Saturday 22nd November
Liverpool (0) 0
Barnsley (1) 1 Ward 35
Att: 41,101   Ref: Winter

Anfield may not have the reputation it used to have, but Liverpool had won five home games on the trot before Ashley Ward went there. The Tykes were outclassed on several occasions this season, but this was one match when they did the outclassing as ten men held out in the second half to collect all three points.

Ashley Ward's goals since his move from Derby have put a £5m price tag on his head

Blackburn Rovers

the rovers

Roy Hodgson, the English manager who doesn't manage the English way, comes to east Lancashire and suddenly Blackburn Rovers have a decent, cohesive side again. Surely they must be contenders?

Selling Shay Given at the end of the last campaign must have seemed a mistake to Rovers' fans in August and a headache to the new manager. The outgoing goalkeeper had left after Kenny Dalglish had guaranteed him a first team place at St James Park, but he would probably have got a shirt at Ewood Park too when Tim Flowers was forced to miss the beginning of the season through injury. In the event, there wasn't a problem; John Filan came in and the Rovers got off to a flying start.

With the keeper protected by new signings Henchoz and Valery, Blackburn were a different team from last year. Both Chris Sutton and Kevin Gallagher were scoring enough goals to send them straight to the top of the table

and the whole team was playing with such panache that the 7-2 defeat of Sheffield Wednesday saw them go 5-1 up in 24 minutes. There was a confidence about the side that had been lacking and now seemed to have been directly instilled back into them by the arrival of their new manager.

"I would be disappointed if we don't reach Europe," Hodgson said when he first arrived at Ewood Park. The incoming manager had a record of success but even coming from him, this seemed optimistic talk for a team that had been far from its Premiership winning best last year. But Hodgson was right. Rovers maintained their early challenge and stayed amongst the leading pack throughout the campaign, despite also losing their stand-in

keeper with a broken arm sustained in that win against Wednesday.

But the coach has had his fair share of help and good luck too. Eire youth international Damien Duff came through this year and has settled well into the team, and Stuart Ripley scored a goal. The winger's strike against West Ham was his first in over three years.

Blackburn Rovers now face European competition next year, where Hodgson's style of play and knowledge of the continental game will stand them in good stead in the UEFA Cup. Rovers aren't the "loadsamoney" club they once were, and they may still be a way short of winning the Premiership again, but it will be a surprise if they don't end up the top six in the league again next season.

CLUB FACTS

Stadium: **Ewood Park** (01254) 698888
Capacity: **31,367**
Manager: **Kenny Dalglish**
Club Captain: **Tim Sherwood**

Premiership record
1992/93 **4th**
1993/94 **2nd**
1994/95 **Champions**
1995/96 **7th**
1996/97 **13th**

TRANSFERS IN

Feb '98	**Callum Davidson**	St Johnstone	£1.75m
Sep '97	**Andreas Andersson**	Malmo FF	£500k
Sep '97	**Alan Fettis**	Nottingham Forest	£300k
Sep '97	**T Pedersen**	St Pauli	£500k
Jul '97	**Martin Dahlin**	Roma	£2.5m
Jun '97	**John Filan**	Coventry	£700k
Jun '97	**Patrick Valery**	Bastiaun	Undisclosed
Jun '97	**Stephane Henchoz**	Hamburg	£3m

TRANSFERS OUT

Mar '98	**Lars Bohinen**	Derby	£1.45m
Dec '97	**Chris Coleman**	Fulham	£2m
Sep '97	**Georgie Donis**	released	free
Sep '97	**Ian Pearce**	West Ham	£2m
Aug '97	**Henning Berg**	Manchester United	£5m
Aug '97	**Graham Fenton**	Leicester	£1.1m
Aug '97	**Graeme Le Saux**	Chelsea	£5m
Jul '97	**Nicky Marker**	Sheffield United	£200k
Jul '97	**Paul Warhurst**	Crystal Palace	£1.25m
Jul '97	**N Gudmundsson**	Malmo FF	£300k
Jul '97	**Matt Holmes**	Charlton	£250k
May '97	**Shay Given**	Newcastle	£1.5m

GAME OF THE SEASON

Saturday 17th January
Blackburn (2) 5 Sherwood, Gallacher (3), Ripley
Aston Villa (0) 0
Att: 24,834   Ref: Burge

This was probably Rovers' best performance since August, the month when they beat Villa 4-0 away, and it re-established them as serious championship contenders. The result came off the back of a disappointing 3-1 defeat at Pride Park, but with Gallacher on fire, Villa again could offer no challenge to Roy Hodgson's team.

Tim Sherwood with Gary Flitcroft. The Rovers captain ended the season by signing a new contract at the club

Bolton Wanderers

the trotters

With 98 points last year, most people thought Bolton the team most likely to stay up. And they were. But that says more about Barnsley and Palace than it does about the Trotters

Bolton began this season in their swanky new £25million Reebok Stadium as they sought to avoid the relegation they suffered last time they were in the Premiership. Bolton won the First Division by a street, in no small part thanks to the goals of Nathan Blake and John McGinlay. It was McGinlay who had narrowly pipped the 22-year-old Blake to the honour of top scorer during the team's Nationwide League success, and although the veteran would not feature so heavily this year, Blake proved himself capable of taking over the mantle of player most likely to score.

The Trotters had also signed Boro right back Neil Cox to bolster the defence, as well as Robbie Elliot and Peter Beardsley to add some class to the midfield. But it quickly became apparent that these three additions to the squad might not be enough, especially when Elliot was lost to a double fracture of his right leg in the match against Everton. But unlike fellow strugglers Spurs and Wimbledon, Bolton cannot blame their struggle this year on their injury list. It is also true that they have lost a number of players to suspension. Bolton have been involved in a number of onfield disagreements with their adversaries over the course of the campaign; the dismissal of their captain Alan Thompson against Blackburn was the team's fifth red card of the season.

Colin Todd brought in Mark Fish and Dean Holdsworth as the club's survival prospects crumbled, but neither made a dramatic difference. The South African took time to become accustomed to the defensive duties of a centre-back in England, while Dean Holdsworth looked an adequate, if uninspired addition to the front line. In the end, it was the surprise signing of West Brom's Bob Taylor that was to be Bolton's best hope of salvation.

It didn't auger well when the new striker missed more than a few against Southampton, but the man who couldn't even get into the West Brom First team was to become an unlikely hero in the Premiership. Though Taylor didn't score in the 5-2 win over Palace, the team did enough to go into their final game at Stamford Bridge with as good a chance as Everton of staying up another year.

CLUB FACTS

Stadium: **The Reebok Stadium**
(01204) 521101
Capacity: **25,000**
Manager: **Colin Todd**
Club captain: **Alan Thompson**

Premiership record
1992/93 **2nd (Div 2)**
1993/94 **14th (Div 1)**
1994/95 **3rd (Div 1)**
1995/96 **20th**
1996/97 **1st (Div 1)**

TRANSFERS IN

Nov '97	**Jussi Jaaskelainen**	VPS Vassa	£100k
Sep '97	**Dean Holdsworth**	Wimbledon	£3.5m
Sep '97	**Mike Whitlow**	Leicester	£500k
Sep '97	**Mark Fish**	Lazio	£2m
Aug '97	**Peter Beardsley**	Newcastle	£450k
Jul '97	**Robbie Elliott**	Newcastle	£2.5m
May '97	**Neil Cox**	Middlesbrough	£1.5m

TRANSFERS OUT

Mar '98	**Peter Beardsley**	Fulham	free
Mar '98	**Jamie Pollock**	Manchester City	£1m
Nov '97	**Steve McAnespie**	Fulham	£100k
Nov '97	**John McGinlay**	Bradford	£625k
Aug '97	**Mixu Paatelainen**	Wolves	£200k

GAME OF THE SEASON

Saturday 2nd May
Bolton Wanderers (3) 5 Blake 7, Fish 20, Phillips 30, Thompson 70, Holdsworth 79
Crystal Palace (2) 2 Gordon 8, Bent 16.
Att: 24,449   Ref: Barry
The crowd sang: "Are you watching Everton?" as the Trotters came back from 2-1 down. Palace were playing for pride and the first half was well contested, but Ron Noades' selection was outplayed in the second half as Bolton escaped the bottom three for the first time since the New Year to battle for survival on the final day.

Alan Thompson's goals and midfield grit have been invaluable to the team in the Nationwide League and in the Premiership

Chelsea

the blues

The FA Cup holders and Charity Shield winners have their sights set on the championship this year, but inconsistency in the league means they have to settle for other silverware

Title-chasing Chelsea had more world class strikers on the bench than most countries have in the whole of their league, but none of them showed the goalscoring form of champions over the entire season this year. Even with Graeme Le Saux back after four years at Blackburn, the defence still looked a little makeshift, as was seen on the first day of the campaign, when the Blues got on the wrong end of a Dion Dublin hat-trick.

Chelsea bounced back from that with Gianluca Vialli hitting four against Barnsley, though even that was not enough to get him into the team for the subsequent four victories, nor to give him so much as a sniff of another international cap. Gianfranco Zola also lost his place in the Italian team this season, but then put himself back into the frame at the last minute when he collected his first hat-trick in English football against Derby. Tore Andre Flo, who will be going to France with Norway, and who is looking a lot better with the ball at his feet than he used to, also scored three against Spurs to contribute to the Blues' heaviest defeat of their London rivals for 62 years.

But the big event of the season at Stamford Bridge was, of course, the departure of Ruud Gullit. No-one seemed to know quite what was going on in Ken Bates' office, least of all Gullit, but the outcome was the appointment of millionaire's son Gianluca Vialli as the new player/manager. Vialli started the job by picking himself for the First team and then justified his place in the side through hard work and goals. But Gullit's favoured Cup player then dropped himself for the Coca-Cola Cup final, saying he had: "every confidence in the players on the pitch." He was right; Chelsea beat Boro 2-0 to become the first English team to claim a UEFA Cup place next year, though by then, the title they coveted was already beyond their reach.

The cost of losing Gustavo Poyet cannot be underestimated; he scored 14 goals from midfield in Spain's *Primera Division* last year and was looking well on course to repeating the feat until he broke his leg. With him back in the side now, Chelsea will expect to pick up some more silverware next year, maybe even the title.

CLUB FACTS	TRANSFERS IN				TRANSFERS OUT			
Stadium: **Stamford Bridge**	Feb '98	**Brian Laudrup**	Rangers	pre-Contract	Jan '98	**Frode Grodas**	Tottenham	£250k
(0171) 385 5545	Aug '97	**Graeme Le Saux**	Blackburn	£5m	Jul '97	**Craig Burley**	Celtic	£2.5m
Capacity: **41,000**	Jun '97	**Bernard Lambourde**	Bordeaux	£1.5m	Jun '97	**Scott Minto**	Benfica	free
Managers: **Ruud Gullit, Gianluca Vialli**	Jun '97	**Ed De Goey**	Feyenoord	£2.25m	May '97	**Erland Johnsen**	Rosenborg	free
Club Captain: **Steve Clarke**	May '97	**Tore Andre Flo**	Brann Bergen	£300k				
	May '97	**Gustavo Poyet**	Zaragoza	free				
Premiership record	May '97	**Celestine Babayaro**	Anderlecht	£2.25m				
1992/93 **11th**								
1993/94 **14th**								
1994/95 **11th**								
1995/96 **11th**								
1996/97 **6th**								

GAME OF THE SEASON

Sunday 5th October
Liverpool (2) 4 Berger 20, 35, 57 Fowler 64
Chelsea (1) 2 Zola 22 Poyet 85 (pen)
Att: 36,647   Ref: Elleray

After an impressive start, Chelsea were brought down to earth at Anfield, where they also lost Bernard Lambourde who was sent off by referee David Elleray. The Premiership program was then postponed for World Cup fixtures, and the Blues were lucky to get a point at Filbert Street when the race resumed. They then lost in Tromso and returned to be beaten at Bolton. Hardly championship form – and the season had just begun.

Sparky Hughes in familiar company, but
the Welsh Wizard is now a Chelsea hero

Coventry

the sky blues

Gordon Strachan inspires the Sky Blues to their best ever Premiership season as Dion Dublin takes over from him as the leader on the pitch, and even plays for England

This has been a season of unexpected joy for Coventry. Traditionally, the Sky Blues escape relegation on the last day of the season, snatching the necessary three points when all around them fail and thereby somehow manage to avoid the drop against all the odds.

This season showed something of a transition, and there is no reason to suppose that the changes won't be permanent. Coventry battled to get something from matches where they would have rolled over and died in previous years. In the spring, the Sky Blues' defenders were the clean-sheet kings of the Premiership.

The difference was, quite simply, the influence of last year's assistant manager and veteran midfielder, Gordon Strachan. He took over full managerial responsibilities from the departing Ron Atkinson over the summer, and instilled a confidence, self-belief and will to win that hasn't been seen at Highfield Road since John Sillett's glory, glory days. His outbursts at referees show just how passionate he is about his football, and that kind of commitment couldn't fail to rub off on his players.

Coventry were without Gary McAllister and Noel Whelan for much of the season, but didn't seem to notice. Darren Huckerby continued to demonstrate what an astute signing he has been since coming from Newcastle the year before. The team assured themselves of another year's Premiership football by the end of February. By then, with 40 points already in the bag, they had even risen into the top half of the table.

The difference under Strachan was that everyone had to fight for their place in the team. Dion Dublin led the line, both in defence and in attack. The new captain scored his 100th goal for the club this season, while Steve Ogrizovic played his 600th League game in the home tie against Derby. The 40-year-old keeper said: "I am feeling as good as ever and my reflexes are still sharp," but he has since given up his jersey to younger blood to take on a coaching role, though he remains a registered player.

Strachan can take Cov' even further next year if he finds a little more creativity in midfield and can keep the players he's got.

CLUB FACTS	TRANSFERS IN			TRANSFERS OUT			
Stadium: **Highfield Road** (01203) 234000	Dec '97	**Viorel Moldovan**	Grasshoppers	£3.25m	Feb '98	**Kyle Lightbourne**	Stoke	£500k
Capacity: **23,662**	Dec '97	**George Boateng**	Feyenoord	£250k	Nov '97	**Brian Borrows**	Swindon	free
Manager: **Gordon Strachan**	Jul '97	**Roland Nilsson**	Helsingborgs	£200k	Sep '97	**Kevin Richardson**	Southampton	£150k
Club captain: **Dion Dublin**	Jul '97	**Martin Johansen**	Copenhagen	£0.5m	Aug '97	**John Filan**	Blackburn	£700k
	Jul '97	**Magnus Hedman**	AIK Solna	free	Jul '97	**Peter Ndlovu**	Birmingham	£1.6m
Premiership record	Jul '97	**Kyle Lightbourne**	Walsall	£500k	Jul '97	**Alex Evtushok**	released	free
1992/93 **15th**	Jun '97	**Trond Soltvedt**	Rosenborg	£500k	Jul '97	**Eoin Jess**	Aberdeen	£700k
1993/94 **11th**	May '97	**Simon Haworth**	Cardiff	£500k	Jun '97	**Iyesden Christie**	Mansfield	free
1994/95 **16th**							
1995/96 **16th**							
1996/97 **17th**							

GAME OF THE SEASON

Sunday 28th December
Coventry (1) 3 Whelan 12, Dublin 86 (pen), Huckerby 88
Man Utd (1) 2 Solskjaer 30, Sheringham 47
Att: 23,054   Ref: Barry

Darren Huckerby's remarkable winner just two minutes after Dion Dublin's equalising penalty, when Huckerby: "probably beat half our team," as Alex Ferguson described it, showed everything that is different about the new Coventry. It was one of the most exciting final five minutes anywhere in the Premiership this season.

Darren Huckerby has come from the
Newcastle reserves to become one of the
most feared strikers in English football

Crystal Palace

the eagles

In a doomed bid to avoid relegation, Palace seemed to buy pretty much anybody with top flight experience who became available to them this year. They even signed Thomas Brolin

Having come straight back up to the Premiership through the play-offs after only finishing sixth in Division One last year, you might have expected Palace fans to consider this season to have been a bonus. But this is a club with lofty aspirations, and despite the money made on Hopkin and Roberts, Palace must have spent just about every penny of their Premiership money on the players they hoped would keep them in the top flight. Ultimately these players did not perform well enough at home to do that. And despite a decent away record, Palace were the first team to be relegated.

The signing of Attilio Lombardo from Juve in the summer overshadowed the arrivals of Kevin Miller and Paul Warhurst. While these latter two would make their contributions during the course of the season, it was Lombardo who was the instant hit with some inspirational performances. The Italian was later joined at Selhurst Park by his former Juve colleague Michele Padovano, though by this time it was the other mid-season signing Neil Shipperley who stole the limelight with five goals in his first four games.

The loss of David Tuttle was a blow, as was Hermann Hreidarsson's debut own goal. But Hreidarsson immediately made amends for that mistake by cutting out the threat of Bergkamp in the next match and then opening his scoring account in the win against Wednesday at Hillsborough.

At that time Palace had the best away record in the league but then in the new year, after Lombardo and Padovano were both lost to injury during the 3-0 home defeat by Liverpool, the team's away form failed them too, and the Eagles dropped towards the relegation zone.

Valerian Ismael and Sasa Curcic did their best to keep their new club up but the Eagles were far too often outclassed by the top sides. A case in point was the final home defeat by Manchester United which saw them mathematically relegated. With the Red Devils still playing for an outside hope of the title, that match was as close to a foregone conclusion as they come. Palace now have the problem of keeping the team together for another promotion attempt from Division One next season.

CLUB FACTS

Stadium: **Selhurst Park (0181) 768 6000**
Capacity: **26,309**
Managers: **Steve Coppell, Attilio Lombardo, Ron Noades**
Club captain: **Attilio Lombardo**

Premiership record
1992/93 20th
1993/94 1st (Div 1)
1994/95 19th
1995/96 3rd (Div 1)
1996/97 6th (Div 1)

TRANSFERS IN

Mar '98	**Sasa Curcic**	Aston Villa	£1m
Feb '98	**Matt Jansen**	Carlisle	£1m
Jan '98	**Marcus Bent**	Brentford	£300k
Jan '98	**Valerien Ismael**	Strasbourg	£2.75m
Jan '98	**Thomas Brolin**	Leeds	free
Nov '97	**Michele Padovano**	Juventus	£1.7m
Oct '97	**Jamie Smith**	Wolves	swap
Aug '97	**Neil Emblem**	Wolves	£1.8m
Jul '97	**Attilio Lombardo**	Juventus	£1.6m
Jul '97	**Paul Warhurst**	Blackburn	£1.5m
Jun '97	**Kevin Miller**	Watford	£1.5m

TRANSFERS OUT

Mar '98	**Neil Emblen**	Wolves	undisclosed
Mar '98	**Andy Roberts**	Wimbledon	£1.6m
Jan '98	**Itzhik Zohar**	released	free
Dec '97	**Gareth Davies**	Reading	£175k
Dec '97	**Carl Veart**	Millwall	£50k
Nov '97	**George Ndah**	Swindon	£500k
Oct '97	**Kevin Muscat**	Wolves	swap
Oct '97	**Douɣie Freedman**	Wolves	swap
Aug '97	**Tony Scully**	Man City	£200k
Jul '97	**David Hopkin**	Leeds	£3.25m
Jun '97	**Chris Day**	Watford	swap
Jun '97	**Ray Houghton**	Reading	free

GAME OF THE SEASON

Saturday 18th April
Crystal Palace (0) 3 Jansen, Curcic, Bent
Derby (0) 1 Bohinen
Att: 18,101   Ref: Alcock

Palace eventually saved themselves from the ignominy of being relegated without winning a single home game when they overcame Derby at Selhurst Park. It was a great team performance and a win that kept them within sight of safety. Bohinen's goal was nothing but a late consolation for the visitors, though in truth it was all about saving face for Palace by then.

Hermann Hreidarsson was discovered by
David "Kid" Jensen's wife in Iceland!

Derby County

the rams

A new ground and a new hope. Periods of form when they are virtually unstoppable at Pride Park establish Derby in the Premiership as the Rams now look for a place in Europe

Derby did themselves proud this year. However, when the Rams kicked off the campaign with Sturridge and Asanovic out injured, there just wasn't enough pride shown in the Rams' performances early on to get results. A season of struggle loomed.

It took until the rather fortunate home win over Barnsley at the end of August for the Rams to earn their first points in the campaign. Two new Italian signings were both very much involved in that result: Stefano Eranio scoring the winner from the penalty spot after Francesco Baiano had seen his initial kick saved and Paul Durkin ordered the penalty to be retaken. It wasn't pretty, but teams who get results without playing well are usually going places, and sure enough, Derby soon began to climb the table and mount a challenge for a UEFA Cup place.

Jon Hunt and Chris Powell both scored their first goals for the club in the win over Everton but the Rams also managed to throw away two goal leads to both Leeds and Manchester Uniteds. Those results exposed the team's defensive frailties and would eventually prove enough to cost them a place in Europe this season. Nevertheless, Derby remained unbeaten at home throughout 1997 and it was their home record over the course of the season that kept them up in contention for a place in the top six right up until May '98.

Jim Smith made some noticeable signings that transformed the side from relegation fodder into a decent mid-table outfit. Baiano, Eranio and Wanchope got the plaudits, but Mart Poom was outstanding in goal and Deon Burton did enough to make it into the Jamaican national team, if not the Rams' First XI. The manager will need a couple more players if his team are to do as well next year, and they are still a long way shy of winning the title as they last did in 1975. Whatever happens now, this season has established the club in the Premiership.

The defence is still prone to off days, but the three-man frontline can be devastating when the rest of the team is playing well. If they can improve on their away record, and keep their runs of home form going for a little longer, the Rams can do just as well again next year as they did over the course of this.

CLUB FACTS

Stadium: **Pride Park** (01332) 667503
Capacity: **30,000**
Manager: **Jim Smith**
Club captain: **Igor Stimac**

Premiership record
1992/93 **8th (Div 1)**
1993/94 **6th (Div 1)**
1994/95 **9th (Div 1)**
1995/96 **2nd (Div 1)**
1996/97 **12th**

TRANSFERS IN

Mar '98	**Lars Bohinen**	Blackburn	£1.45m
Feb '98	**Rory Delap**	Carlisle	£500k
Aug '97	**Deon Burton**	Portsmouth	£1m
Jul '97	**Francesco Baiano**	Fiorentina	£650k
May '97	**Jonathon Hunt**	Birmingham	£750k
May '97	**Stefano Eranio**	AC Milan	free

TRANSFERS OUT

Jan '98	**Matt Carbon**	WBA	£800k
Dec '97	**Aljosa Asanovic**	Napoli	£500k
Nov '97	**Paul Trollope**	Fulham	£600k
Nov '97	**Paul Simpson**	Wolves	£75k
Sep '97	**Ashley Ward**	Barnsley	£1.3m
Aug '97	**Sean Flynn**	WBA	£260k
Aug '97	**Kevin Cooper**	Stockport	£150k
Jun '97	**Marco Gabbiadini**	released	free
Jun '97	**Steve Hayward**	Fulham	tribunal
Jun '97	**Martin Taylor**	Wycombe	free
Jun '97	**Darren Wassell**	Birmingham	£150k
Jun '97	**Paul McGrath**	released	free

GAME OF THE SEASON

Saturday 1st November
Derby (0) 3 Wanchope 46, 65, Sturridge 82,
Arsenal (0) 0
Att: 30,004   Ref: Alcock

Carling's Player of the Month for October, Paulo Wanchope, began November by destroying Arsenal's unbeaten record. Jim Smith had made four changes to the team that had lost 4-0 at Anfield the previous week, and it took Ian Wright's missed penalty before the Rams took control. After that it was all Derby and Wanchope. Dean Sturridge added the third just before the end.

Francesco Baiano's demonic appearance
does jutice to his style and flair

Everton

the toffeemen

As if last season wasn't bad enough, Howard Kendall marks his return by trading experienced internationals for Nationwide League stalwarts. They win the Merseyside derby... but that's about all

This season was one of unmitigated disaster for the Toffeemen. After a summer of promises from chairman Peter Johnson concerning the appointment of a top coach, or failing that, former player and Sky TV pundit Andy Gray, Howard Kendall began his third stint as Everton boss. It seemed a desperate measure. Kendall took the team to European and domestic glory in the 1980s, but his record since then is poor. The team resorts to long balls to Duncan Ferguson as confidence fades.

Andy Hinchcliffe returned from a longterm knee injury against Derby only to be sent off with the game already lost. Neville Southall, the best goalkeeper the club, and perhaps the country, has ever seen, had a terminal dip in form. Former players Kevin

Richardson and Dave Jones return with Southampton to win 2-0. Howard Kendall called for a "dogs of war spirit" but this proved as elusive as any phantom. Everton found themselves only goal difference away from the drop zone as autumn turned to winter.

It got worse... not only did Everton suffer five consecutive defeats and then went four games without scoring, so the fans called for Johnson to stand down as chairman.

There was light at the end of the tunnel when Duncan Ferguson returned from a ban to net a hat-trick of headers against Bolton, but the season had already degenerated into a fight for Premiership survival.

The only New Year cheer was the promise of teenagers John Oster,

Michael Ball, and in particular, the stylish Danny Cadamarteri.

Finally, Nick Barmby and Duncan Ferguson started playing like the footballers they are. Everton won three out of four, albeit one against Palace at Selhurst Park, where Barmby scored his first in three months and Frenchman Mickael Madar scored on his debut. The Toffeemen came from behind to beat Chelsea, and moved up to 13th place. They battled for a draw at Upton Park, but ominously, Gary Speed was not on the team coach for London that day. Speculation this time became fact and in February, Speed followed Hinchcliffe out of Goodison Park. As a result, Everton began to look a couple of internationals short of a Premiership side again.

PREMIERSHIP WINNERS

CLUB FACTS
Stadium: Goodison Park (0151) 330 2200
Capacity: **40,200**
Manager: **Howard Kendall**
Club Captain: **Dave Watson**

Premiership record
1992/93 **13th**
1993/94 **17th**
1994/95 **15th**
1995/96 **6th**
1996/97 **15th**

TRANSFERS IN
Feb '98	Don Hutchison	Sheffield United	£1m
Jan '98	John O'Kane	Man Utd	£400k
Dec '97	Mickael Madar	Deportivo LC	free
Nov '97	Thomas Myhre	Stavanger	£800k
Nov '97	Carl Tiler	Sheffield United	swap
Nov '97	Mitch Ward	Sheffield United	swap
Aug '97	Danny Williamson	West Ham	swap
Aug '97	Tony Thomas	Tranmere	£400k
Jul '97	John Oster	Grimsby	£1.5m
Jul '97	Gareth Farrelly	Aston Villa	£700k
May '97	Slaven Bilic	West Ham	£4.5m

TRANSFERS OUT
Mar '98	Neville Southall	Stoke	free
Feb '98	Jon O'Connor	Sheffield United	swap
Feb '98	Gary Speed	Newcastle	£5.5m
Jan '98	Andy Hinchcliffe	Sheffield Wed	£3m
Nov '97	Graeme Stuart	Sheffield United	swap
Aug '97	David Unsworth	West Ham	swap

GAME OF THE SEASON
Saturday 18th October
Everton (1) 2 Ruddock (og) 45, Cadamarteri 75
Liverpool (0) 0
Att: 40,112   Ref: Reed

It may have been a dreadful year, but at least the Toffeemen beat Liverpool. Everton went into the game on the back of a poor performance against Wednesday but this time Ferguson won everything that was lofted his way. A Hinchcliffe corner was headed on by Speed for the first and Danny Cadamarteri's low drive made this the third successive game in which the youngster had scored. A period of optimism followed.

Everton have a rare celebration during a season in hell for the Toffeemen

Leeds United
the whites, the peacocks

Modest improvement for the Yorkshire United as manager George Graham capitalises on the workmanlike defence he created in 1996-97 with a solid midfield and Jimmy Floyd Hasselbaink

L eeds continued to move in the right direction under George Graham with three midfield signings including one of the best-value buys of the season, Bruno Ribeiro – they all did well. Tony Yeboah returned to Germany, having failed to build on impressive performances when he first arrived. However, replacement Jimmy Floyd Hasselbaink scored on his debut. The big difference was the form of Rod Wallace. The former Saints man played up front this year and went straight to the top of the Premiership goalscoring charts, kicking off with two at Hillsborough in the second match of the campaign, a game in which Ribeiro also got onto the score sheet.

It was soon clear that there was still a way to go before the club could expect to win the championship they last claimed in 1992.

The alarm bells sounded when Leeds lost their eight-month unbeaten home record to Crystal Palace. Then Leicester recorded their first victory at Elland Road in 17 years. An impressive display against champions Manchester United, capped by David Wetherall leaping above Gary Pallister to head home the winner, was followed by a 4-1 thrashing of Newcastle. Three successive comebacks then set the fans' hearts pounding. Against Derby, from 3-0 down, Leeds took all the points with a last-minute Lee Bowyer winner. Then they did the same thing at Elland Road with three goals in the last quarter of an hour. The next week, they did it again in the derby with Barnsley having gone 2-0 down inside half an hour. George Graham was Manager of the Month for November but celebrations were tempered by news of the death of Leeds' legend, Billy Bremner.

The new year showed the same variable form until Leeds hit a rich vein that included a 5-0 demolition of Derby. It was "same old Leeds" at Upton Park on March 30th but the comprehensive 3-0 defeat, and indeed the whole season, was put into perspective when the plane carrying the squad back to Yorkshire from Stansted airport was forced to abandon take-off when one of its engines caught fire. Fortunately no one was hurt. Leeds can now look forward to Europe with a strong, if still uninspired and uninspiring, team.

CLUB FACTS

Stadium: **Elland Road (0113) 271 6037**
Capacity: **40,000**
Manager: **George Graham**
Club captain: **David Hopkin**

Premiership record
1992/93 **17th**
1993/94 **5th**
1994/95 **5th**
1995/96 **13th**
1996/97 **11th**

TRANSFERS IN

Feb '98	**Martin Hiden**	Rapid Vienna	£1.3m
Aug '97	**Bruno Ribeiro**	Setubal	£500k
Jul '97	**David Hopkin**	Crystal Palace	£3.25m
Jun '97	**Alfie Haaland**	Forest	£1.6m
Jun '97	**Jimmy Hasselbaink**	Boavista	£2m
May '97	**David Robertson**	Rangers	£500k

TRANSFERS OUT

Mar '98	**Richard Jobson**	Manchester City	free
Jan '98	**Tomas Brolin**	Crystal Palace	free
Jan '98	**Pierre Laurent**	Bastia	£500k
Sep '97	**Carlton Palmer**	Southampton	£1m
Sep '97	**Tony Yeboah**	Hamburg	£1m
Aug '97	**Tony Dorigo**	Torino	free
Aug '97	**John Pemberton**	released	free
Aug '97	**Ian Rush**	Newcastle	free
Jul '97	**Brian Deane**	Sheffield United	£1m
Jul '97	**Mark Ford**	Burnley	£250k
Jul '97	**Andy Couzens**	Carlisle	£100k

GAME OF THE SEASON

Saturday 4th October
Coventry (0) 0
Leeds (0) 0
Att: 17,770   Ref: Wilkie

The scene of George Graham's first match in charge after replacing Howard Wilkinson 13 months before. Leeds didn't win this year either but the commitment Graham felt was missing when they lost last year's corresponding fixture 2-1 was very much in evidence; it gave the team the confidence to earn some tough results in the autumn and keep them in contention for Europe.

Jimmy Floyd Hasselbaink is always likely to net a few but never likely to remain quiet

Leicester

the foxes

Martin O'Neill's gritty side build upon the impressive campaign that brought them the Coca-Cola Cup last year and with it the chance of European football

Despite what looked a testing start to the campaign after selling the effective Simon Grayson, Leicester started with a win over their Midlands rivals, Aston Villa. That was followed by a 2-1 win at Anfield and draws at home against Manchester United and Arsenal. The subsequent win over Spurs left the Foxes placed for a return to Europe in 1998-99 after going out of the UEFA Cup to two late Atletico Madrid strikes at the Vicente Calderon.

But trouble was brewing. Steve Claridge expressed his frustration at not getting enough first-team action and was put on the transfer list. Then the holders were put out of the Coca-Cola Cup by Grimsby Town, having disposed of Sheffield Wednesday in the second round. French keeper Pegguy Arpaxhed came into the team to good effect, though he made his debut on the losing side at Stamford Bridge.

Leicester went back into fourth place with a win over West Ham to keep their UEFA Cup place hopes alive. Their first win in 21 years at Highfield Road then kept them sixth.

Soon after he was sent off in injury time for raising his fists at St James Park, Emile Heskey was involved in transfer speculation. An unfortunate defeat at Highbury then left O'Neill conceding: "We need a few more decent players to keep us alive."

Tony Cottee returned from a loan spell at Birmingham City but the Foxes ended the year by dropping two points to 10-man Sheffield Wednesday. Leicester were ninth, and two points short of O'Neill's stated target of 30 for the new year.

After being dumped out of the FA Cup by beleagured Crystal Palace, Leicester held their ground in the league. They were even linked with Dion Dublin and Stoke City defender Andrew Griffin before the transfer deadline. Dublin, however, would stay at Highfield Road, while Griffin signed for Newcastle. Leicester signed Theo Zagorakis instead and spent the rest of the season in the top half.

Although in the end it wasn't quite enough to get them back into Europe, Martin O'Neill has shown that it is possible to build a good Premiership side, and one that is capable of competing as equals in Europe, without breaking the bank.

CLUB FACTS

Stadium: **Filbert Street (0116) 291 5000**
Capacity: **22,517**
Manager: **Martin O'Neill**
Club captain: **Matt Elliot**

Premiership record
1992/93 **6th (Div 1)**
1993/94 **4th (Div 1)**
1994/95 **21st**
1995/96 **5th (Div 1)**
1996/97 **9th**

TRANSFERS IN

Feb '98	**Theo Zagorakis**	PAOK	£750k
Aug '97	**Pegguy Arphaxed**	RC Lens	free
Aug '97	**Tony Cottee**	Selangor	£0.5m
Aug '97	**Graham Fenton**	Blackburn	£1.1m
Jul '97	**Rob Savage**	Crewe	£400k

TRANSFERS OUT

Sep '97	**Mike Whitlow**	Bolton	£0.5m
Jun '97	**Simon Grayson**	Aston Villa	£1.35m
Jun '97	**Neil Lewis**	Peterborough	£60k
Jun '97	**Jamie Lawrence**	Bradford	£50k

GAME OF THE SEASON

Wednesday 27th August
Leicester (0) 3 Heskey 84, Elliot 90, Walsh 90
Arsenal (1) 3 Bergkamp 9, 61, 90
Att: 21,089 Ref: Barber

O'Neill's men appeared to be on to a loser when they found themselves 2-0 behind with only seven minutes remaining. Goals from Heskey and Elliot looked like earning a remarkable draw, but then Bergkamp completed his hat-trick to put Arsenal back in the lead in injury time. A last gasp Steve Walsh header gave Leicester the draw they had fought for and deserved.

Emile Heskey beats Rio Ferdinand to the ball. In future years, these two may well be England teammates.

Liverpool

the reds

First place is the only place for Reds' fans. It's not that they lost the Premiership that has upset them this season, it's the way they lost it. The emergence of Michael Owen offers hope though

Liverpool's success in the '70s and '80s was built on a flat 4-4-2 formation. They now alternate between this and Roy Evans' favoured wingback system, but still seem to get more results whenever they revert to type. Then there's the trouble they've been having at the back. Mark Wright's experience might be lacking, and David James' loss of form hasn't helped, but games have been lost before the final whistle and the only improvements this season have been in attack.

After 40 goals in the reserves last season, Michael Owen equalised from the spot on his debut, and despite his manager's contention that he: "couldn't be expected to last the whole season," the youngster not only did that but also got into the England team. With

European Cup winner Karl-Heinz Riedle signing over the summer as well, Liverpool looked to have got the front line sorted. But although Riedle broke his duck in the win over Leeds, that was Liverpool's first win of the season.

Paul Ince scored on his home debut against Leicester but didn't live up to the expectations made of him after his return to form at Inter. There were also criticisms that Leonhardsen was being played out of position on the left.

Off the field, McManaman flew to Barcelona on a wild goose chase and there were also rumours that Jason McAteer might be on his way too. With Leonhardsen and Fowler out injured, the prospects for glory looked slim. But after the defeat in Strasbourg, Evans reverted to a 4-4-2 against Derby and

won 4-0. The win over Palace was also achieved with four at the back. The Reds then beat Coventry, Leeds and Newcastle and eventually got a work permit for Brad Friedel.

Liverpool were then knocked out of the FA Cup by Coventry but their League form did improve. Then it all started to fall apart again.

Liverpool had by then all but qualified for next year's UEFA Cup, but their fans want to win the title every year and they don't like to see their team give up on that. The way the players celebrated the draw with Man United that effectively cost United the title tells its own story. Even Roy Evans ended the season complaining of his team's failure to battle for results.

CLUB FACTS	TRANSFERS IN			TRANSFERS OUT			
Stadium: **Anfield** (0151) 263 2361	Dec '97	**Brad Friedel**	Colombus Crew	£1m	Mar '98	**Mark Kennedy**	Wimbledon	£1.75m
Capacity: **45,000**	Dec '97	**Haukua Gudnason**	Keflavik	£150k	Dec '97	**Jason Jones**	Swansea	free
Manager: **Roy Evans**	Jul '97	**Karlheinz Riedle**	Dortmund	£1.8m	Nov '97	**Paul Dalglish**	Newcastle	free
Club captain: **Paul Ince**	Jul '97	**Paul Ince**	Inter Milan	£4.2m	Aug '97	**John Barnes**	Newcastle	free
	Jul '97	**Danny Murphy**	Crewe	£3m	Jun '97	**Lee Jones**	Tranmere	£100k
Premiership record	Jun '97	**Oyvind Leonhardsen**	Wimbledon	£4m	May '97	**Stan Collymore**	Villa	£7m
1992/93 **6th**								
1993/94 **8th**								
1994/95 **4th**								
1995/96 **3rd**								
1996/97 **4th**								

GAME OF THE SEASON

Saturday 28th March
Barnsley (1) 2 Redfearn 37 (pen), 85
Liverpool (1) 3 Riedle 44, 59, McManaman 90
Att: 18,684   Ref: Willard

Liverpool could have conceded five by half time but after Barnard and Morgan were sent off for fouls on Owen, Riedle's 30-yarder in between times looked the winner. Then Redfearn's late equaliser meant Liverpool had to fight for it, if only against eight men after Sheridan walked, again after an incident involving Owen. McManaman then scored the winner and Gary Willard had to be escorted down the tunnel after the final whistle.

As well as being a great provider,
Stevie McManaman found his
scoring boots this year.

Manchester United

the red devils

Disappointment in every competition for the team seeking its third successive title, but the Red Devils still qualify for the 1998-99 Champions League, despite conceding the Premiership to Arsenal

H aving lost Eric Cantona to retirement over the summer and Roy Keane to injury against Leeds in September, it is a credit to the Man United squad that they still spent most of the season as clear favourites for the Championship. Indeed, for quite a while it looked a foregone conclusion that they would win it.

Alex Ferguson now has a large enough squad of players to cover any gaps. The signing of Teddy Sheringham was one of the most astute of the season, as the England man seamlessly took on Cantona's role. With the likes of Nicky Butt and Paul Scholes in midfield, Roy Keane was scarcely missed. But it has taken the manager a long time to get his squad into its current shape. For the first few years of

his tenure there were criticisms about his spending a lot of money without bringing honours to Manchester, but the club is very much back on keel again these days after some difficult times in the last 25 years. The performance of their up-and-coming youngsters is testament to the dynasty that Ferguson has built at Old Trafford and a warning for the future.

The form of the team in autumn and mid-winter was such that by New Year, nobody expected them not to win the title. Although everyone knows that championships are not decided that soon, 1998 looked to be the exception to that rule as the Red Devils started to put more and more clear water between themselves and their nearest rivals with some devastating performances. But

when they did start to slip in the spring, Arsenal took full advantage and eventually won the league with two games left to play. And so the Lancashire United went into the Roses match against Leeds already knowing that they were only playing for pride.

There was to be no silverware for the Old Trafford faithful this year, but Alex Ferguson was magnanimous in defeat, saying that Arsenal: "deserved to win it after the way they've done the business like that." Peter Schmeichel added: "We must look on the positive side of all this and take on board all the lessons which must be learned and use them in a constructive manner for next season." It seems that Manchester United will try to win everything in sight then too.

CLUB FACTS	TRANSFERS IN			TRANSFERS OUT			
Stadium: **Old Trafford (0161) 872 1661**	Aug '97	**Henning Berg**	Blackburn	£5m	Jan '98	**John O'Kane**	Everton	£400k
Capacity: **56,387**	Jun '97	**Teddy Sheringham**	Spurs	£3.5m	Dec '97	**Karel Poborsky**	Benfica	£2m
Manager: **Alex Ferguson**	May '97	**Erik Nevland**	Viking Stavanger	Free	Aug '97	**Michael Appleton**	Preston	£500k
Club captain: **Roy Keane**					Aug '97	**Simon Davies**	Luton	£150k
					Jul '97	**Pat McGibbon**	Wigan	£200k
Premiership record					May '97	**Eric Cantona**	retired	
1992/93 **Champions**								
1993/94 **Champions**								
1994/95 **2nd**								
1995/96 **Champions**								
1996/97 **Champions**								

GAME OF THE SEASON

Saturday 25th October

Man Utd (4) 7 Cole 17, 19, 45, Giggs 43, 56, Scholes 59, Poborsky 80

Barnsley (0) 0

Att: 55,142   Ref: Riley

It may be known as the Theatre of Dreams for Manchester United fans, but Old Trafford was the Theatre of Nightmares for any team facing the Champions there in the first half of this season. Barnsley's first visit in 60 years saw Andy Cole find his form and Ryan Giggs score two brilliant goals. The Red machine was unstoppable. Barnsley must have wished they'd never been promoted.

David Beckham: a season of ups and downs domestically and for England

Newcastle United

the magpies

Newcastle have seen the resignation of two members of the board this year after comments they made about the fans, but it's the problems on the pitch that are paramount for Geordies

They say the Newcastle defence has improved under Kenny Dalglish, but you wouldn't know it on the basis of this year. Alessandro Pistone slotted in well on the left hand side, defending stoically and getting forward into attacking positions, but the back line as a whole has too often been as shaky as it ever was under Kevin Keegan.

In those days, Newcastle relied on the simple tactic of scoring more goals than the opposition, but having already sold Les Ferdinand in the summer, not to mention Peter Beardsley, Lee Clark and David Ginola, the Mags were left acutely short of attacking options when Shearer was injured in late July. But that was just the start of it. Newcastle have had what Rob Lee called: "the worst injury list I've ever known." In the captain's opinion: "even a club the size of Newcastle finds that difficult to cope with."

The main worries were up front after Shearer was lost. "The Les Ferdinand deal was a good one on the Thursday we agreed to it," said then-chairman Freddie Shepherd. "We had Shearer and Asprilla, and Tomasson had come in and was looking good." Tomasson was top scorer in the Dutch league last year for Herenveen, but although he scored goals pre-season, he failed to prove a replacement for Shearer. Faustino Asprilla was sporadically special, but when he was sidelined in the autumn, and with Temuri Ketsbaia yet to score in the Premiership, John Barnes found himself playing as first choice striker. Barnes has played up front before, but Newcastle still lacked a striker who, as Lee put it: "could score on the break after you've soaked up pressure."

Dalglish resisted the temptation to panic buy and waited to sign Swedish international Andreas Andersson in the New Year. Of the earlier signings, John Barnes, Stuart Pearce and Ian Rush had all shown over the course of the season that they were still perfectly capable of playing in the Premiership. But they are all dependable squad players nowadays rather than the catalysts who can transform an average team into a good one. And Newcastle were average. So they had to wait for their saviour Shearer to return to rescue them from the dreaded drop.

CLUB FACTS

Stadium: **St James Park (0191) 201 8400**
Capacity: **36,610**
Manager: **Kenny Dalglish**
Club captain: **Rob Lee**

Premiership record
1992/93 **(Div 1 Champions)**
1993/94 **3rd**
1994/95 **6th**
1995/96 **2nd**
1996/97 **2nd**

TRANSFERS IN

Mar '98	**Paul Robinson**	Darlington	£250k
Mar '98	**James Coppinger**	Darlington	£250k
Mar '98	**Nicos Dabizas**	Olympiakos	£2m
Feb '98	**Stephen Glass**	Aberdeen	pre-Contract
Feb '98	**Gary Speed**	Everton	£5.5m
Jan '98	**Andrew Griffin**	Stoke	£1.5m
Jan '98	**Anders Andersson**	AC Milan	£3m
Aug '97	**Ian Rush**	Leeds	Free
Aug '97	**John Barnes**	Liverpool	Free
Jul '97	**Alessandro Pistone**	Inter Milan	£4.3m
Jul '97	**Stuart Pearce**	Forest	Free
Jul '97	**Temuri Ketsbaia**	AEK Athens	Free
Jun '97	**Bjarni Gudjonsson**	IA Arkanes	£500k
May '97	**Shay Given**	Blackburn	£1.5m
May '97	**Jon Dahl Tomasson**	Heerenveen	£2.5m

TRANSFERS OUT

Feb '98	**John Beresford**	Southampton	£1.5m
Jan '98	**Faustino Asprilla**	Parma	£6.1m
Aug '97	**Peter Beardsley**	Bolton	£450k
Jul '97	**Les Ferdinand**	Tottenham	£6m
Jul '97	**David Ginola**	Tottenham	£2m
Jul '97	**Robbie Elliott**	Bolton	£2.5m
Jun '97	**Lee Clark**	Sunderland	£2.5m

GAME OF THE SEASON

Monday 13th April
Newcastle (1) 2 Andersson 40, Shearer 86
Barnsley (0) 1 Fjortoft 50
Att: 36,534   Ref: Dunn

Newcastle collect all three points when Alan Shearer exposes Barnsley's habit of losing late goals with his header. The visitors had deserved a point, but the result kept the Magpies out of the drop zone at a critical point in the season. It also showed exactly why Alan Shearer is so important to the team.

Newcastle United: so much was expected, so little delivered. At least Shearer's back

Sheffield Wednesday
the owls

Wednesday may have finished last year as the best placed team in Yorkshire but few people fancied them to challenge as closely for a UEFA Cup place this year

David Pleat was a successful and popular manager when he replaced Trevor Francis but the signings of Patrick Blondeau and Paolo Di Canio over the summer didn't set hearts racing in Yorkshire any more than they did in the rest of the football world.

Owls' fans had been promised a new cavalry charge from the Sheffield Wednesday band, to be played whenever the team broke out of defence. But that wasn't so often this year. Wednesday got off to such a dreadful start that fans were already calling for Pleat to be replaced as manager by the time of the draw at Villa Park. Subsequent defeats to fellow strugglers Spurs and Palace then left the Owls deep in the bottom three. Di Canio forged a good relationship with

his compatriot Carbone, the star of the team, but with Atherton, Hyde and Booth injured, and without Mark Pembridge's goals, they were always in for a tough ride. As for Blondeau, Arsenal had already bought the best of Monaco's Championship winning defence and the right-back returned to France before the season was out, having aired his differences.

On the pitch, Wednesday were lucky to lose 7-2 to Blackburn, and within a week of the 6-1 defeat at Old Trafford, Pleat was out of a job.

Ron Atkinson, who had taken the team to promotion and won the League Cup in 1991, came back to replace Pleat, and Wednesday's home form began to improve. But it was Pleat-signing Petter Rudi who was the

revelation, at least when he was fit.

Wednesday beat Arsenal in Big Ron's first game back in charge. This result was followed by a trip to Southampton, where another certainty of football occurred; David Hirst, the Saints' record signing, scored against his old club. But it was Di Canio who won the match with a goal six minutes from time.

Wednesday battled and began to look half the team they had been the previous season as they recorded their fourth successive win, this time against Barnsley. That run ended with defeat at Upton Park, but Wednesday remained unbeaten until February. Although Wednesday stayed clear of the danger zone, this wasn't the season Owls' fans had hoped for.

CLUB FACTS	TRANSFERS IN				TRANSFERS OUT			
Stadium: **Hillsborough** (0114) 221 2121	Feb '98	**Earl Barrett**	Everton	free	Mar '98	**O'Neill Donaldson**	Stoke	free
Capacity: **39,859**	Feb '98	**Goce Sedloski**	Hadjuk Split	£750k	Jan '98	**Adem Poric**	Rotherham	monthly
Managers: **David Pleat, Ron Atkinson**	Jan '98	**Andy Hinchcliffe**	Everton	£3m	Jan '98	**Wayne Collins**	Fulham	£500k
Club captain: **Peter Atherton**	Oct '97	**Petter Rudi**	Molde	£800k	Jan '98	**Patrick Blondeau**	Bordeaux	£1.2m
	Sep '97	**Bruce Grobbelaar**	Oxford	nominal	Oct '98	**David Hirst**	Southampton	£2m
Premiership record	Sep '97	**Jim Magilton**	Southampton	£1.6m	Jun '97	**Regi Blinker**	Celtic	swap
1992/93 **7th**	Aug '97	**Paolo Di Canio**	Celtic	£3m	May '97	**Orlando Trustfull**	V Arnhem	£800k
1993/94 **7th**	Jun '97	**Patrick Blondeau**	Monaco	£1.8m	May '97	**Michael Williams**	Burnley	free
1994/95 **13th**					May '97	**Brian Linighan**	released	free
1995/96 **15th**								
1996/97 **7th**								

GAME OF THE SEASON

Saturday 8th November
Sheff Wed (5) 5 Booth 29, 33, 44, Di Canio 20, Whittingham 26
Bolton (0) 0
Att: 25,027   Ref: Reed

It is a certainty of football that a team will always win after a managerial change. It happened against Arsenal in Big Ron's first match back in charge, but the 5-0 thrashing of Bolton in the week when Peter Shreeves took over as caretaker from David Pleat was some backlash. Petter Rudi was outstanding and the entire team received a standing ovation after the performance from their previously critical fans.

Paolo Di Canio: new boots and plaudits
from the Wednesday faithful

Southampton

the saints

With a new manager whose only pedigree was taking Stockport into the First Division last year, and with Le Tissier out with a broken arm, Southampton started the season as favourites to go down

When Dave Jones was in charge at Stockport County, the young manager would apparently visit Alex Ferguson for tea and football chat. He obviously picked up some tips because this season the pupil beat the master. The home win over Manchester United was the Saints' third successive Premiership victory over Ferguson's side at the Dell. They beat them 3-1 in 1995-96 and 6-3 in 1996-97 when Manchester United blamed the colour of their shirts for their poor first-half performance. This time, it wasn't such a shock, and it showed just how far Southampton had come.

The campaign had seemed all over before it had even begun when the Saints lost five of their opening six games, with the Graeme Souness signing Kevin Davies getting their only winning goal against Palace on his second game in the team. Le Tissier came back for the Liverpool game, but had to be substituted just before halftime with hamstring trouble as things went from bad to worse. It wasn't until October, when Carlton Palmer and David Hirst came into the squad, that the results started to improve. Palmer held the midfield together while Hirst went one better than Davies by scoring twice in the 3-2 win against Spurs in his second game for the club.

Jones wasn't afraid to drop Le Tissier for away matches whenever he felt the team needed more bite in midfield. The manager has also shown that he is capable of breathing life back into some highly talented but out-of-form signings. "I knew exactly what I was getting into here," said Jones. "And the players had expected a big name to take charge, so I had to prove myself to them as much as they had to prove themselves with me."

Rather than face another relegation battle, after this season's showing, the fans will be hoping their team can regain the form they were showing at the beginning of the '80s when they reached their highest ever league position of third place.

They'll also want Francis Benali to score again. The full-back's goal against Leicester was his first ever for the club, while his sending off in the home fixture against Derby was the 11th red card of career.

CLUB FACTS

Stadium: **The Dell (01703) 220505**
Capacity: **15,000**
Manager: **David Jones**
Club captain: **Matt Le Tissier**

Premiership record
1992/93 18th
1993/94 18th
1994/95 10th
1995/96 17th
1996/97 16th

TRANSFERS IN

Feb '98	**John Beresford**	Newcastle	£1.5m
Oct '97	**David Hirst**	Sheff W	£2m
Sep '97	**Carlton Palmer**	Leeds	£1m
Sep '97	**Jason Bowen**	Birmingham	£550k
Sep '97	**Kevin Richardson**	Coventry	£150k
Aug '97	**S Johansen**	Bodo-Glimt	£600k
Jul '97	**Paul Jones & Lee Todd**	Stockport	£1.7m
Jun '97	**Kevin Davies**	Chesterfield	£750k

TRANSFERS OUT

Mar '98	**Robbie Slater**	Wolves	£50k
Jan '98	**Simon Charlton**	Birmingham	£200k
Nov '97	**Maik Taylor**	Fulham	£700k
Nov '97	**Alan Neilson**	Fulham	£250k
Oct '97	**Neil Maddison**	Middlesbrough	£250k
Oct '97	**Mickey Evans**	WBA	£750k
Oct '97	**Barry Venison**	retired	N/A
Oct '97	**Christer Warren**	Bournemouth	Undisclosed
Sep '97	**Jim Magilton**	Sheff W	£1.6m
Jul '97	**Ulrich Van Gobbel**	Feyenoord	£800k
Jun '97	**Eyal Berkovic**	West Ham	£1.75m

GAME OF THE SEASON

Saturday 25th April
West Ham (1) 2 Sinclair 42, Lomas 82
Southampton (1) 4 Le Tissier 40, Ostenstad 63 86, Palmer 80
Att: 25,878 Ref: Gallagher

Matt Le Tissier opened the scoring after getting on to the rebound when his first shot hit the post. Ostenstad hit two, while "Palmer was magnificent" in his manager's words. West Ham "defended badly and were punished," as Harry Redknapp commented afterwards. But on the day, the difference was that Southampton were by far the better of these two up and coming sides.

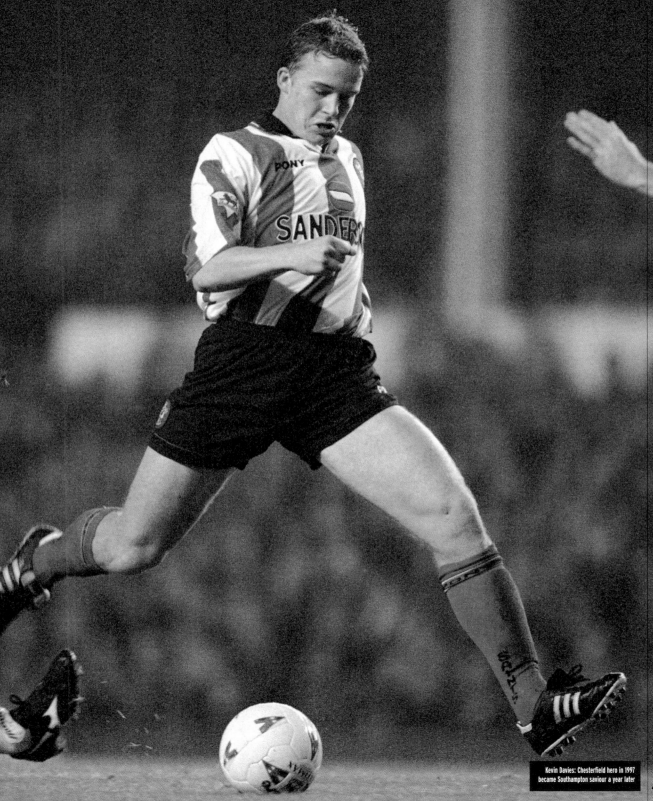

Kevin Davies: Chesterfield hero in 1997
became Southampton saviour a year later

Tottenham Hotspur

spurs

Tottenham narrowly avoid relegation. With a fully fit squad, they would undoubtedly have made mincemeat of the First Division, but when was the last time Spurs had a fully fit squad?

H aving been at White Hart Lane for three years, manager Gerry Francis understood from the outset that: "this is a big club, the supporters come every week and want success." He would have known that if he couldn't put together a winning team from whoever wasn't on the physio's couch, he would be out of a job. He didn't succeed, and when the fans saw no joy by November, Christian Gross and his assistant Fritz Schid were drafted in from Grasshoppers of Zurich to replace him at the helm.

They found they had inherited a promising wing partnership in José Domingues and David Ginola, two players signed by Gerry Francis, but also that the makeshift defence wasn't performing. Christian Gross immediately followed his predecessor in commenting

on the paramount need to get results. "We are at the bottom and we need points." But the new manager's first experience of life in London was watching Palace win 1-0 at White Hart Lane from the stands. There was training the next day.

There was no improvement over Christmas as the world began to realise that some of the greatest clubs in English football history will struggle if the size of the Premiership is trimmed. By the New Year, Spurs looked a good bet for the drop.

Understandably, when the opportunity arose, Christian Gross signed Jürgen Klinsmann back to the club on six months' loan from Sampdoria. Many, however, suspected that Klinsmann was past his best; he

was out of the national side and his club form was one of the reasons why Samp' had let him go. The question wasn't resolved for a while as Klinsmann was injured soon after his arrival. This stroke of bad luck cemented the thought that Spurs might actually get relegated. The fans had to wait until May to see Klinsmann save the day.

After the life-saving Wimbledon game Klinsmann said: "Today was certainly one of the most exciting of my career in 16 years as a professional. It was a wonderful feeling."

This from a man who has won the World Cup. Ecitement aside, he steadfastly refused to discuss his future; he remembers what happened last time.

CLUB FACTS

Stadium: **White Hart Lane**
   (0181) 365 5000
Capacity: **33,208**
Managers: **Gerry Francis,**
   Christian Gross
Club captain: **Gary Mabbutt**

Premiership record
1992/93 **8th**
1993/94 **15th**
1994/95 **7th**
1995/96 **8th**
1996/97 **10th**

TRANSFERS IN

Feb '98	**Moussa Saib**	Valencia	£2.3m
Jan '98	**Frode Grodas**	Chelsea	250k
Jan '98	**Nicola Berti**	Inter Milan	free
Dec '97	**Jürgen Klinsmann**	Sampdoria	loan
Aug '97	**Jose Domingues**	Sporting Lisbon	£1.6m
Jul '97	**Les Ferdinand**	Newcastle	£6m
Jul '97	**David Ginola**	Newcastle	£2m

TRANSFERS OUT

Sep '97	**Jason Dozzell**	Ipswich	free
Aug '97	**Ronny Rosenthal**	Watford	free
Aug '97	**David Kerslake**	Ipswich	free
Jun '97	**Teddy Sheringham**	Manchester Utd	£3.5m

GAME OF THE SEASON

Tuesday 5th May
Wimbledon (2) 2 Fear 21, 30
Tottenham Hotspur (2) 6 Ferdinand 18,
Klinsmann 41, 54, 58, 60, Saib 79
Att: 25,820   Ref: Barber 2/1

Three goals in five minutes from Klinsmann early in the second half put this match well beyond Wimbledon. It left the Dons still with the mathematical possibility of going down, while taking Spurs to safety. Klinsmann capped his performance by setting up Algerian substitute Moussa Saib to complete the scoring.

Jürgen Klinsmann: Alan Sugar's car won't be cleaned with Jürgen's shirt this time

West Ham United
the hammers, the irons

In all, the English press linked the Hammers with 15 players over the close season, but only Eyal Berkovic and Craig Forrest signed, so Redknapp gets some bargains mid-season instead

It didn't look good for West Ham when both Stuart Pearce and John Barnes elected to join Newcastle after being linked with the Irons. Pearce has since said that he had the choice, and that choice was Newcastle, but John Barnes has admitted that he was: "very close to joining West Ham."

But Eyal Berkovic and Craig Forrest did sign. And Berkovic, who was good at Southampton, has gone from strength to strength since his move to London. His fee made him the most expensive Israeli player ever, but it was always going to be another bargain for Redknapp by Premiership standards. Meanwhile, Craig Forrest would have to share the goalkeeper's shirt with a succession of rivals, with Bernard Lama the final instalment in the saga. The former French international keeper's days in London looked numbered when he didn't get straight into the team after French national coach Aime Jacquet had said: "if he does not play before the end of the month, it is hard to see how he can be fit for the finals." But after an aborted return home, where he failed to find a club, his performances for the Irons since then must surely put him back in the reckoning for the World Cup.

Frank Lampard Jnr got his first senior goal in the win at Oakwell on the first day. David Unsworth, a player the press never commented on in the summer, was then paraded to the fans before the win over Spurs at Upton Park. But it was John Hartson's prolific goalscoring that lifted the team towards the top of the table at the start of the season.

Hartson was joined in the West Ham front line by the 24-year-old Ivory Coast-born, French striker Samassi Abou and QPR's Trevor Sinclair. Both showed glimpses of immense talent, and Harry Redknapp has a reputation for making good signings. The Irons didn't quite do enough this term to get into Europe, but there is no reason to suspect that they won't be well up in the top half for most of next season.

A lot may depend on Rio Ferdinand, who needs to become more dependable at the back. He'll get the chance to learn, though. The new England sweeper has now signed a contract that will keep him at Upton Park for a further seven years.

CLUB FACTS

Stadium: Upton Park (0181) 548 2748
Capacity: 25,985
Manager: **Harry Redknapp**
Club captain: **Julian Dicks**

Premiership record
1992/93 **2nd (Div 1)**
1993/94 **13th**
1994/95 **14th**
1995/96 **10th**
1996/97 **14th**

TRANSFERS IN

Jan '98	**Trevor Sinclair**	QPR	£2.3m
Oct '97	**Samassi Abou**	Cannes	£400k
Sep '97	**Andrew Impey**	QPR	£1.2m
Sep '97	**Ian Pearce**	Blackburn	£2m
Aug '97	**David Unsworth**	Everton	swap
Jul '97	**Craig Forrest**	Ipswich	£500k
Jun '97	**Eyal Berkovic**	Southampton	£1.75m

TRANSFERS OUT

Mar '98	**Les Sealey**	Bury	free
Mar '98	**Ian Bishop**	Manchester City	free
Jan '98	**Iain Dowie**	QPR	swap
Jan '98	**Keith Rowland**	QPR	swap
Sep '97	**Michael Hughes**	Wimbledon	£1.6m
Sep '97	**Marc Rieper**	Celtic	£1.5m
Aug '97	**Danny Williamson**	Everton	swap
May '97	**Slaven Bilic**	Everton	£4.5m

GAME OF THE SEASON

Monday 30th March
West Ham (2) 3 Hartson 8, Abou 23, Pearce 68
Leeds United (0) 0
Att: 24,107   Ref: A B Wilkie

West Ham went seventh with this result over their rivals for a UEFA Cup place and the scoreline did not flatter the home side. Although Bernard Lama was called into action more than once, if Nigel Martyn hadn't been in such good form, the score could have been doubled. The game, however, will be remebered for the near disaster on the Leeds' plane back to Yorkshire after the game

John Hartson : when he was good he was very, very good, but when he was bad...

Wimbledon

the dons

Rumours of a move to Dublin obscured the Dons' tough battle to stay in the top flight as the floodlights go out on them twice... at Pride Park and at Selhurst Park

Everyone expects the Dons to struggle, but they rarely do. They've looked more like qualifying for Europe than being relegated in recent years, so this season was a turnaround in form and personnel for the gypsies. And not just because the chairman wanted the club to move to Dublin.

It began when Joe Kinnear sold Oyvind Leonhardsen despite his assertion that the Dane was: "One of the best players I ever signed" which makes him quite a signing. His replacement Ceri Hughes, signed for one tenth of Leonhardsen's fee, was made sub for his first game against Liverpool. After that draw, the Selhurst Park squatters began looking like they would end their remarkable record in the top flight.

Then another youngster came through the ranks. Carl Cort's debut goal earned the points at Newcastle where he looked effective beside Jason Euell. "The boy can play," Kinnear enthused after the game. "He has good feet and is very mature for his age." Kinnear then announced in the New Year that he had £5million to spend. This was useful; nine first team players were out for the trip to Sheffield. But then the only signings Kinnear made before the transfer deadline were Andy Roberts from landlords Palace, and Charlton's out-of-favour target man Carl Leaburn, who promptly started scoring goals.

There had been speculation early in the season over Liverpool's Republic of Ireland international winger Mark Kennedy, but the asking price of

£3million had proved too rich then; it would have dramatically cut the profit made on Leonhardsen. And when Dean Holdsworth left for Bolton, Kinnear said: "I must have sold £30million worth of players in my seven years at the club and if Deano goes it will be good business." It was, and the team kept a lot of clean sheets in the Spring, though they didn't ensure their survival until after Easter. Meanwhile, off the park, plans to build a new stadium near Plough Lane fell through. Sam Hammam asked fans to: "be patient." But he knew they wouldn't go to Dublin. The latest rumour concerns the city of Hull. That's a long way from south east London too. But Wimbledon are certain to remain tenants at Selhurst Park, at least until next season.

CLUB FACTS

Stadium: **Selhurst Park** (0181) 771 2233
Capacity: **26,309**
Manager: **Joe Kinnear**
Club captain: **Robbie Earle**

Premiership record
1992/93 **12th**
1993/94 **6th**
1994/95 **9th**
1995/96 **14th**
1996/97 **8th**

TRANSFERS IN

Mar '98	**Mark Kennedy**	Liverpool	£1.75m
Mar '98	**Andy Roberts**	C Palace	£1.2m
Jan '98	**Carl Leaburn**	Charlton	£300k
Oct '97	**Stalle Solbakken**	Lillestrom	£225k
Sep '97	**Michael Hughes**	West Ham	£800k
Jul '97	**Ceri Hughes**	Luton	£400k

TRANSFERS OUT

Mar '98	**Vinnie Jones**	Q.P.R.	£500k
Oct '97	**Dean Holdsworth**	Bolton	£3.5m
Jun '97	**Aidan Newhouse**	Fulham	Free
Jun '97	**Oyvind Leonhardsen**	Liverpool	£4.5m

GAME OF THE SEASON

Saturday 22nd November
Wimbledon (0) 2 Ardley 68, M. Hughes 70
Manchester United (0) 5 Butt 48, Beckham 66, 76,
Scholes 81, Cole 87.
Att: 26,309 Ref: Durkin

A 2-0 lead is surrendered and the fans chant: "We'll never go to Dublin." But Sam Hammam tells them after the match he wants the move if Merton council can't find the space. Hammam also denies that Egil Olsen will join the Dons after the World Cup, insisting that the Norwegian national coach was at the game only: "to watch the four Norwegians who were involved."

Neil Sullivan's rich form in goal for the
Dons earned him a Scotland call-up

Welcome to the other
COMPETITIONS

While Sky TV's exhaustive coverage of the English Premiership has led many fans to believe it the only competition worth fighting for, our most successful teams trod foreign soil, while the teams from the Nationwide League enjoyed their chance to upset the big boys in the Coca-Cola Cup. And who would join the Premiership from Division One?

Manchester United and Newcastle were England's representatives in Europe's most prestigious competition, the Champions' League. Newcastle's star shone bright when they met Barcelona at St James Park, Tino Asprilla completing a glorious hat-trick, but for Dalglish's men, it was to be the highlight of their campaign. Manchester United came close again, but were eliminated on the away-goals rule by Monaco in the quarter-final. Despite four English teams competing in the UEFA Cup, only Aston Villa progressed as far as the last eight, but Chelsea reached the final of the Cup Winners' Cup. They also guaranteed a place in Europe next season by winning the Coca-Cola Cup, while Nottingham Forest and Middlebrough regained their Premiership places automatically.

CUP WINNERS' CUP

Domestic cup winners from across Europe enter the Cup Winners' Cup. It's the easiest European trophy to win because many of the teams involved can be fairly weak

12

UEFA CUP

Formerly known as the Fairs Cup, this is the competition for teams who placed in the top five or six in their domestic league. So it's not an easy cup to win though...

14

CHAMPIONS' LEAGUE

The Uniteds of Manchester and Newcastle were the English entrants to this season's Champions' League. But once again, it was not to be...

16

LEAGUE CUP

Now the Coca-Cola Cup, it's still worth a place in the UEFA Cup for the victors, despite the reticence of some clubs to take it seriously. Vialli likes it though...

18

DIVISON ONE

The Premiership is the Holy Grail for Division One clubs, with teams clawing desperately for the top two automatic promotion places. Welcome back Forest and Boro...

20

CUP WINNERS' CUP

1997-1998

Chelsea have shown their cup pedigree by winning the FA Cup and the Coca-Cola Cup in the last two seasons. And this time around, Gianluca Vialli's men reached the final of the Cup Winner's Cup...

Despite Chelsea manager Gianluca Vialli's assertion that he wants to win the Premiership above everything else, it was in the European Cup Winners' Cup that he and his team excelled this season. Chelsea lost far too many games in the league at Stamford Bridge to challenge for anything other than a UEFA Cup place.

Former Blues' boss Ruud Gullit preferred Vialli to his other strikers for the first two rounds, and with Frank Sinclair and Graeme Le Saux out for the home leg against Bratislava, Danny Granville and Paul Hughes replaced them in the full-back positions. The youngsters kept a clean sheet and ten minutes from time, Hughes crossed for Granville to head home his first goal for the club. Chelsea repeated the result in Slovakia, Vialli scoring the second when keeper Miroslav Konig's attempted clearance rebounded off the Italian and back into his net. It was a bitterly cold night in Slovakia and that goal must have stung Vialli as much as it stunned

the keeper. But the weather was nothing compared to what waited for Chelsea 350 miles north of the Arctic Circle in frozen Norway.

Chelsea had already conceded three goals before the heavy snow began to fall at half-time, but Gianluca Vialli bagged a brace after the interval to give Chelsea two vital away goals. If Roberto Di Matteo hadn't been alert early in the return match at Stamford Bridge, Chelsea might have conceded an early goal. But with Tromso setting their stall out to defend from deep, Chelsea were given far too much room to attack and they rattled seven past the Norwegians. Vialli helped himself to a hat-trick and Petrescu scored twice.

Chelsea then went to the other end of Europe to play Betis in Seville. Tore Andre Flo, the former-Tromso man who was on the bench for the game against his old club, scored two stunning individual efforts. Although Alfonso pulled one back, Chelsea held on to take a one goal advantage back to

England. The two away goals gave Chelsea the option to attack in the home leg and they went through to the semi-final quite comfortably against a Betis side whose league form had not been up to par, either.

Vicenza in the semi-final away were quite a different proposition. They battled for the ball and Chelsea were constantly forced to scramble in their own half, while Schenardi, Zauli, Luisi and Ambrosetti picked up on every mistake, of which there were several. When Vicenza scored an early away goal in the return match, it seemed all over, but this was a night of cold rain and glory for veteran striker Mark Hughes. The Welshman, who had been the man left out for Vialli in the first game of the competition, came on for the last 20 minutes to volley the goal that put Chelsea into the final against VfB Stuttgart. After that game, Vialli said: "We are nearly ready to be the best team in England." Next season, he wants the Premiership.

DATE	TEAMS & GAME	SCORES	GOAL SCORERS		REFEREE	CARDS
18/9/97 1ST ROUND	Chelsea v Slovan Bratislava	2 0	Di Matteo, Granville		R Boggi (Italy)	5 0
2/10/97	Slovan Bratislava v Chelsea	0 2	Di Matteo, Vialli	(Chelsea win 4-0 on aggregate)	A Hamer (Luxembourg)	3 0
23/10/97 2ND ROUND	Tromso IL v Chelsea	3 2	S Nilsen, Fermann, Arst Vialli (2)		J Granat (Poland)	1 0
6/11/97	Chelsea v Tromso IL	7 1	Petrescu (2), Vialli (3), Zola, Leboeuf (pen) B Johansen	(Chelsea win 9-4 on aggregate)	V Melnichuk (Ukraine)	1 1

DATE	TEAMS & GAME	SCORES	GOAL SCORERS		REFEREE	CARDS
5/3/98 QUARTER FINAL	Real Betis v Chelsea	1 2	Alfonso Flo (2)		A Ouzounov (Bulgaria)	0 0
19/3/98	Chelsea v Real Betis	3 1	Sinclair, Di Matteo, Zola George	(Chelsea win 5-2 on aggregate)	B Heynemann (Germany)	3 0
2/4/98 SEMI FINAL	Vicenza v Chelsea	1 0	Zauli Poyet, Zola, M. Hughes		M Diaz Vega (Spain)	5 0
16/4/98	Chelsea v Vicenza	3 1	Bosanovich, Bosanovich Luiso	(Chelsea win 3-2 on aggregate)	Marc Batta (France)	1 1

Dennis Wise displays his famous cheeky grin as he lifts the FA Cup in 1997

UEFA CUP

1997-1998

Atletico Madrid see off Leicester and end Villa's excellent run, while Liverpool and Arsenal fail to live up to the fans' expectations after their previous successes in European competition...

With the exception of Villa, there was little cheer for English clubs in the UEFA Cup. Leicester and Arsenal both fell at the first hurdle, though the Foxes can consider themselves unlucky after getting on the wrong end of a couple of questionable refereeing decisions. Poor Liverpool were destroyed in Strasbourg.

Leicester went out when, after having taken an early lead against Atletico Madrid, they conceded a dubious penalty. And Martin O'Neill's men were furious when Muzzy Izzet was denied what looked a clear penalty decision in their favour at Filbert Street. It was a tough introduction to European competition.

Arsenal had no excuses. Bergkamp missed the trip to the intimidating atmosphere of PAOK Salonika's Toumba stadium because his fear of flying. Despite Tony Adams' return to the team, Arsenal lost. Adams then picked up his second yellow card of the tie at Highbury to rule him out of the first European tie of next season.

Liverpool won the "Battle of Britain" with a dramatic last minute goal at Celtic Park from Steve McManaman ("probably as good a goal as I've ever scored"). Macca surged forward from within his own half to hit a tremendous shot. Celtic probably deserved a win on the night and could have won the second leg after some uncomfortable goalkeeping from David James, but the Reds marched on.

Meanwhile, Savo Milosevic made Bordeaux whine with only nine minutes of extra time remaining. The Villans then disposed of Athletic Bilbao, though there were tense moments after the Basques reduced the deficit at Villa Park to come within one goal of an aggregate win.

Liverpool were then mauled in Alsace by Strasbourg, though after the 3-0 Cup Winners' Cup defeat at the Parc des Princes last year, they should have known better. It could have been a lot worse too, and Liverpool fans who complain that their team lacks a will to win point to this match as evidence. "It's the same old story, and it's driving me round the bend," complained Evans. The Reds were much better in the second leg but the deficit proved too much despite a second goal five minutes from time.

DATE	TEAMS & GAME	SCORES	GOAL SCORERS		REFEREE	CARDS	
16/9/97	Atletico Madrid v Leicester	2 1	Juninho, Vieri (pen) Marshall		R H Olson (Norway)	2 0	
30/9/97	Leicester v Atletico Madrid	0 2	Juninho, Kiko (Atletico win 4-1 on aggregate)		R Harrel (France)	1 2	
16/9/97	Bordeaux v Aston Villa	0 0			A Ancion (Belgium)	2 0	
30/9/97	Aston Villa v Bordeaux	1 0	Milosevic (Villa win 1-0 on aggregate)		K E Fisker (Denmark)	2 0	
16/9/97	Celtic v Liverpool	2 2	McNamara, Donnelly (pen) Owen, McManaman		C Graziano (Italy)	3 0	
30/9/97	Liverpool v Celtic	0 0	(Liverpool win 2-2 on away goal rule)		E Steinborn (Germany)	3 0	
16/9/97	PAOK Salonika v Arsenal	1 0	Fratzeskos		M Diaz Vega (Spain)	8 0	
30/9/97	Arsenal v PAOK Salonika	1 1	Bergkamp Vrizas (PAOK win 2-1 on aggregate)		M Piraux (Belgium)	4 0	

DATE	TEAMS & GAME	SCORES	GOAL SCORERS		REFEREE	CARDS	
21/10/97 2nd Round	Athletic Bilbao v Aston Villa	0 0			H Strampe Germany	2 0	
4/11/97	Aston Villa v Athletic Bilbao	2 1	Taylor, Yorke Gonzalez (Villa win 2-1 on aggregate)		S Piller (Hungary)	3 0	
21/10/97	Strasbourg v Liverpool	3 0	Zitelli (2), Conteh		M Pereira (Portugal)	1 0	
4/11/98	Liverpool v Strasbourg	2 0	Fowler (pen), Riedle (Strasbourg win 3-2 on aggregate)		R Pedersen (Norway)	3 0	
25/11/97 3rd Round	Steaua Bucharest v Aston Villa	2 1	Oakes (og), Ciocoiu Yorke		L Michel (Hungary)	1 0	
9/12/98	Aston Villa v Steaua Bucharest	2 0	Milosevic, Taylor (Villa win 3-2 on aggregate)		B Heynemann (Germany)	1 0	
3/3/98 Q-Final	Atletico Madrid v Aston Villa	1 0	Vieri (pen)		S Braschi (Italy)	6 0	
17/3/98	Aston Villa v Atletico Madrid	2 1	Taylor, Collymore Caminero (Madrid win on away goal rule)		M Van Der Ende (Holland)	3 0	

Arsenal's dynamic Dutchman Dennis
Bergkamp fires home against Salonika

Steve McManaman breaks Celtic hearts
with a stunning individual effort

Stan Collymore and Aston Villa fall to
Atletico Madrid on the away-goals rule

PREMIERSHIP WINNERS

55

CHAMPIONS' LEAGUE

1997-1998

The Uniteds fail to bring the European Cup back to England, but there are enough positive signs in some of their displays to show that they can compete with the best...

Manchester United, as champions, and Newcastle United as the Premiership's second placed team, qualified to represent England in the European Champions' League this year. But England will have to wait at least one more season to see if one of its clubs can lift the continent's most coveted trophy again.

There were highlights however. Andy Cole collected a hat-trick as Man Utd won their first five games to come within one match of making a clean sweep of the group stages – a feat that only AC Milan, PSG and Spartak Moscow have achieved. Cole scored five goals in six games in a run that included a hard fought win over the competition favourites, Juventus, to threaten the

Italians' chances of making the quarter-finals. They then made light work of Feyenoord and Kosice, both home and way. Those results were not so highly regarded at the time, but they were put into perspective when Juventus did not find those ties quite so easy.

But the defeat in Turin in the final game allowed the Old Lady of Italian *calcio* back into the competition. Man Utd's subsequent failure to press for a goal in Monaco in the quarter-finals proved the Red Devils' downfall, before they could meet the Italians again. Alex Ferguson blamed Monaco's pitch saying: "We would have loved to have played attractive football but that just wasn't possible." But Fergie's caution meant that when the French champions

took an early lead at Old Trafford, it was enough to end his dream of Champions' League glory, if only for another year.

Newcastle too began the campaign in style with a win over Barcelona that was rather more convincing than the final scoreline suggests. Faustino Asprilla was unstoppable in giving his team the three goal lead that killed the tie. And although the Catalans pulled back two late goals, they never looked like equalising.

The Geordies then came back from 2-0 down in Kiev to earn a point before slipping up twice against PSV. Those losses meant that the defeat in the Camp Nou effectively ended their European campaign.

DATE	TEAMS & GAME	SCORES	GOAL SCORERS	REFEREE	CARDS
13/8/97 QUALIFYING	Newcastle v NK Croatia Zagreb	2 1	Beresford (2) Cvitanovic	Krompl (Czech Republic)	3 0
27/8/97	NK Croatia Zagreb v Newcastle	2 2	D Simic, Cvitanovic Asprilla (pen), Ketsbaia	Urs Meier (Sweden)	2 1
17/9/97 GROUP B	FC Kosice v Manchester United	0 3	Irwin, Berg, Cole	L Sundell (Sweden)	0 0
17/9/97 GROUP C	Newcastle v Barcelona	3 2	Asprilla (3, 1 pen) Luis Enrique, Figo	P Collina (Italy)	2 0
1/10/97 GROUP B	Manchester United v Juventus	3 2	Sheringham, Scholes, Giggs Del Piero, Zidane	A Lopez Nieto (Spain)	5 1
1/10/97 GROUP C	Dynamo Kiev v Newcastle	2 2	Rebrov, Shevchenko Beresford (2)	P Mikkelsen (Denmark)	1 0
22/10/97 GROUP B	Manchester United v Feyenoord	2 1	Scholes, Irwin (pen) Vos	S Muhmenthaler (Switzerland)	1 0
22/10/97 GROUP C	PSV Eindhoven v Newcastle	1 0	Jonk	S Braschi (Italy)	7 0
5/11/97 GROUP B	Feyenoord v Manchester United	1 3	Korneev Cole (3)	S Puhl (Hungary)	3 0
5/11/97 GROUP C	Newcastle v PSV Eindhoven	0 2	Nilis, De Bilde	B Gunter (Austria)	3 0

DATE	TEAMS & GAME	SCORES	GOAL SCORERS	REFEREE	CARDS
26/11/97 GROUP B	Manchester United v FC Kosice	3 0	Cole, Faktor (og), Sheringham	A Cakar (Turkey)	0 0
26/11/97 GROUP C	Barcelona v Newcastle	1 0	Giovanni	M Batta (France)	0 0
10/12/97 GROUP B	Juventus v Manchester United	1 0	Inzaghi	G Veissiere (France)	2 0
10/12/97 GROUP C	Newcastle v Dynamo Kiev	2 0	Barnes, Pearce	H Krug (Germany)	3 0

FINAL GROUP B TABLE

Man Utd	6	5	0	1	14	5	15
Juventus	6	4	0	2	12	8	12
Feyenoord	6	3	0	3	8	10	9
FC Kosice	6	0	0	6	2	13	0

(Man Utd and Juventus qualify for the quarter-finals)

FINAL GROUP C TABLE

Dynamo Kiev	6	3	2	1	13	6	11
PSV Eindhoven	6	2	3	1	9	8	9
Newcastle	6	2	1	3	7	8	7
Barcelona	6	1	2	3	7	14	5

(Dynamo and PSV qualify for the quarter-finals)

DATE	TEAMS & GAME	SCORES	GOAL SCORERS	REFEREE	CARDS
4/3/98 Q-FINAL	Monaco v Manchester United	0 0		M Diaz Vega (Spain)	0 0
18/3/98	Manchester United v Monaco	1 1	Solskjaer Trezeguet (Man Utd lose 1-1 on away goals rule)	H Krug (Germany)	4 0

Tino Asprilla scored a hat-trick against
Barcelona before returning to Parma

Coca-Cola Cup

1997-1998

Gianluca Vialli's appointment as Chelsea manager was one of the main stories of the season. Just five weeks later his cosmopolitan Chelsea side won the Coca-Cola Cup...

C helsea and Middlesbrough met in the Coca-Cola Cup final in a repeat of last season's FA Cup showdown at Wembley. And once again, it was heartbreak for Bryan Robson's men as they lost their third cup final in 12 months. Chelsea strode the lush Wembley turf and convincingly outplayed a Middlesbrough team which included Paul Gascoigne for the first time since his transfer from Glasgow Rangers. Frank Sinclair scored the first for Chelsea before Italian international Roberto Di Matteo ensured that Chelsea would at least qualify for the UEFA Cup next season, without having to worry how they performed in other competitions. However, at the start of the competition, UEFA had still not confirmed whether a European place

would be open to the winners of the competition. Indeed, it wasn't until the quarter-final stages that the issue was settled and for many Premiership managers, the decision came too late for them to take the cup seriously.

This season saw only two Premiership clubs get knocked out in the second round. Sheffield Wednesday went out to Grimsby Town, while Crystal Palace lost over two legs to Hull City. Wimbledon, meanwhile, made easy work of their south London derby with Millwall, disposing of the Lions by 9-2 over the two games before they went out to Bolton in the third round.

One of the biggest shocks in the competition was Leeds' defeat by struggling Nationwide outfit Reading. Of the other Premiership clubs 0who

didn't make it to the fourth round, all were put out by their Premiership peers. Leicester City lost 3-1 at Grimsby, and Manchester United were beaten 2-0 at Portman Road by Ipswich Town. Not that Alex Ferguson lost a lot of sleep over that one, particularly with a Champions' League game looming the week after. He is alleged to have said to reporters after the defeat by Ipswich: "Gentlemen, I think you will agree that that was a tremendous result for Manchester United football club." Ferguson feels his team should be allowed to exclude themselves from the cup, leaving them free to concentrate their efforts elsewhere.

But with Chelsea winning the cup, it has guaranteed English clubs an extra UEFA Cup spot for the coming season.

DATE	TEAMS & GAME	SCORES	GOAL SCORERS	REFEREE	CARDS
18/11/98 4th Round	Arsenal v Coventry	1 0	Bergkamp	G R Ashby	4 0
18/11/98	Derby v Newcastle	0 1	Tomasson	M J Bodenham	4 0
18/11/98	Leeds v Reading	2 3	Wetherall Asaba, Morley, Williams	G P Barber	3 0
18/11/98	Liverpool v Grimsby	3 0	Owen (3, 1 pen)	R Pearson	3 0
18/11/98	Middlesbrough v Bolton	2 1	Summerbell, Hignett Thompson	S J Lodge	6 1
18/11/98	Oxford Utd v Ipswich	1 2	Beauchamp Dozzell, Mowbray	S W Mathieson	3 0
19/11/97	Chelsea v Southampton	2 1	Flo, Morris Davies	D R Elleray	2 0
19/11/97	West Ham v Walsall	4 1	Lampard (3), Hartson Watson	D Orr	1 0

DATE	TEAMS & GAME	SCORES	GOAL SCORERS	REFEREE	CARDS
6/1/98 Q-finals	Reading v Middlesbrough	0 1	Hignett	G Cain	2 0
6/1/98	West Ham v Arsenal	1 2	Abou Wright, Overmars	G P Barber	1 2
7/1/98	Ipswich v Chelsea	2 2	Taricco, Mathie Flo, Le Saux (Chelsea win 4-1 on penalties)	P A Durkin	2 0
7/1/98	Newcastle v Liverpool	0 2	Owen, Fowler	D Gallagher	3 0
27/1/98 Semi-finals	Liverpool v Middlesbrough	2 1	Redknapp, Fowler Merson	G S Willard	6 0
28/1/98	Arsenal v Chelsea	2 1	Overmars, Hughes M Hughes	M J Bodenham	4 0
18/2/98	Chelsea v Arsenal	3 1	M Hughes, Di Matteo, Petrescu Bergkamp (pen) (Chelsea win 4-3 on aggregate)	G Poll	9 1
18/2/98	Middlesbrough v Liverpool	2 0	Merson (pen), Branca (Middlesbrough win 3-2 on aggregate)	P A Durkin	5 0
29/3/98 Final	Chelsea v Middlesbrough	2 0	Sinclair, Di Matteo	P Jones	6 0

Chelsea's Coca-Cola Cup win ensured them a European place without league worries

DIVISON ONE

1997-1998

With a place in the Premiership offering enormous financial muscle to clubs, the scrap to win one of the automatic promotion places was a hot as ever. Hats off to Nottingham Forest and Middlesbrough

The introduction of play-offs for the third promotion place means that the season has effectively been extended for many Nationwide League clubs. With the knowledge that sixth place in Division One takes a team to within two wins of the Premiership, any club in the top half of the table is still in the running for a promotion place until well into the New Year. And with goals scored separating teams on the same number of points, rather than goal difference as is used in the Premiership, attacking teams are given a slight advantage over effective but dull also-rans. The system provides more interest but has also been accused of being unfair. Crystal Palace, for example, won promotion last season despite finishing sixth, five points behind third placed Wolverhampton Wanderers. This season, West Bromwich

Albion had a good go of making a challenge early on, as did Swindon Town, before a dramatic decline in form saw the West Country club looking fearfully over their shoulder towards the other end of the table as the campaign came to an end. The big surprise was Stockport County, who had just won promotion from Division Two under Dave Jones, now manager of Southampton. Stockport started astonishingly well and stayed in the top six until the New Year.

However, with clubs the size of Middlesbrough, Nottingham Forest and Sunderland having come back down with their pockets full of Premiership money, it was always going to be hard for any less wealthy club to challenge the big three.

By Easter, the final top six had taken shape. Birmingham City were still

in with a slim chance, but Wolves were as good as out of it, while West Brom and Stockport had well and truly fallen out of the frame. It had come down to the race everyone expected it to be at the start of the season, with the three relegated clubs setting the pace, followed by a chasing pack of clubs with relatively recent experience of the top flight.

Charlton Athletic manager Alan Curbishley had commented at the start of the season, that he believed if clubs like his didn't go up within the next couple of years, they never would. The south London club spent big (by their standards) to try to achieve this goal, but despite a great season at the Valley, the Addicks had to settle for a play-off place. And Sunderland's defeat at Ipswich meant they missed out on automatic promotion as well.

NATIONWIDE LEAGUE TOP SIX		
Forest	46	94
Middlesbro'	46	91
Sunderland	46	90
Charlton	46	88
Ipswich	46	83
Sheff Utd	46	74

Forest and Sunderland are automatically promoted, the remaining clubs play off for the single other Premiership place.

NATIONWIDE LEAGUE TOP GOAL SCORERS	[only includes league goals scored]		
Pierre van Hooijdonk	(Forest)	29	
Kevin Phillips	(Sunderland)	29	
David Johnson	(Ipswich)	25	(8 for Bury)
Kevin Campbell	(Forest)	23	
Clive Mendonca	(Charlton)	23	
Shaun Goater	(Man City)	20	

Pierre van Hooijdonk's tally for the season including cup competitions was 34. Kevin Phillips got 33, Johnson 30, Mendonca 25, Campbell 23 and Brett Angell 23. They play eight more matches in a First Division season than their Premiership counterparts.

Pierre van Hooijdonk could well be playing in the Premiership next season – though probably not with Forest.

MONTH BY MONTH GUIDE TO THE PREMIERSHIP

Starting here is the guide to every game played (excluding abandoned games) in the Premiership this season. You'll find the date of the game played, the scorers, the referee for the game and the number of yellow and red cards shown. This is your essential reference guide to the 1997/1998 season, the dry facts behind the passionate tussle to be crowned Champions of the most exciting league in world football

DATE	TEAMS & GAME	SCORES	GOAL SCORERS	REFEREE	CARDS
9/8/97	Barnsley v West Ham	(1) 1 / (0) 2	Redfearn / Hartson, Lampard	A B Wilkie	2 / 0
9/8/97	Blackburn v Derby	(1) 1 / (0) 0	Gallacher	D R Elleray	0 / 0
9/8/97	Coventry v Chelsea	(1) 3 / (1) 2	Dublin (3) / Sinclair, Flo	P A Durkin	6 / 0
9/8/97	Everton v Crystal Palace	(0) 1 / (1) 2	Ferguson / Lombardo ,Dyer (pen)	S W Dunn	7 / 0
9/8/97	Leeds v Arsenal	(1) 1 / (1) 1	Hasselbaink / Wright	D J Gallagher	4 / 0
9/8/97	Leicester v Aston Villa	(1) 1 / (0) 0	Marshall	S J Lodge	1 / 0
9/8/97	Newcastle v Sheffield Wednesday	(1) 2 / (1) 1	Asprilla (2) / Carbone	P Jones	5 / 0
9/8/97	Southampton v Bolton	(0) 0 / (1) 1	Blake	M J Bodenham	3 / 0
9/8/97	Wimbledon v Liverpool	(0) 1 / (0) 1	Gayle / Owen (pen)	G S Willard	4 / 0
10/8/97	Tottenham v Manchester United	(0) 0 / (0) 2	Butt, Vega (og)	G Pole	4 / 0
11/8/97	Arsenal v Coventry	(1) 2 / (0) 0	Wright (2)	K W Burge	4 / 0
12/8/97	Crystal Palace v Barnsley	(0) 0 / (0) 1	Redfearn	N Barry	2 / 0
13/8/97	Aston Villa v Blackburn	(0) 0 / (3) 4	Sutton (3), Gallacher	P E Alcock	4 / 0
13/8/97	Liverpool v Leicester	(0) 1 / (1) 2	Ince / Elliot, Fenton	J T Winter	2 / 0
13/8/97	Manchester United v Southampton	(0) 1 / (0) 0	Beckham	G P Barber	4 / 0
13/8/97	Sheffield Wednesday v Leeds	(0) 1 / (2) 3	Hyde / Wallace (2), Ribeiro	P A Durkin	6 / 0
13/8/97	West Ham v Tottenham	(1) 2 / (0) 1	Hartson, Berkovic / Ferdinand	S J Lodge	3 / 0
23/8/97	Blackburn v Liverpool	(0) 1 / (0) 1	Dahlin / Owen	S J Lodge	2 / 0
23/8/97	Coventry v Bolton	(2) 2 / (0) 2	Telfer, Huckerby / Blake (2)	M A Riley	5 / 0
23/8/97	Everton v West Ham	(0) 2 / (1) 1	Speed, Stuart / Watson (og)	P Jones	6 / 0
23/8/97	Leeds v Crystal Palace	(0) 0 / (1) 2	Lombardo, Warhurst	U D Rennie	3 / 0
23/8/97	Leicester v Manchester United	(0) 0 / (0) 0		D J Gallagher	0 / 0
23/8/97	Newcastle v Aston Villa	(1) 1 / (0) 0	Beresford	G S Willard	5 / 1
23/8/97	Southampton Arsenal	(1) 1 / (1) 3	Maddison / Overmars, Bergkamp (2)	D R Elleray	4 / 0
23/8/97	Tottenham v Derby	(1) 1 / (0) 0	Calderwood	M J Bodenham	6 / 0
23/8/97	Wimbledon v Sheffield Wednesday	(1) 1 / (0) 1	Euell / Di Canio	A B Wilkie	1 / 0
24/8/97	Barnsley v Chelsea	(0) 0 / (3) 6	Petrescu, Poyet, Vialli (4)	G Pole	1 / 0
25/8/97	Blackburn v Sheffield Wednesday	(5) 7 / (1) 2	Gallacher (2), Hyde (og), Sutton (2), Wilcox, Bohinen / Carbone (2)	J T Winter	3 / 1
26/8/97	Leeds United v Liverpool	(0) 0 / (1) 2	McManaman, Riedle	A B Wilkie	5 / 0
27/8/97	Barnsley v Bolton	(1) 2 / (1) 1	Tinkler, Hristov / Beardsley	D J Gallagher	3 / 0
27/8/97	Coventry v West Ham	(1) 1 / (0) 1	Huckerby / Kitson	N S Barry	4 / 0
27/8/97	Everton v Manchester United	(0) 0 / (1) 2	Beckham, Sheringham	K W Burge	0 / 0
27/8/97	Leicester v Arsenal	(0) 3 / (1) 3	Heskey, Elliot, Walsh / Bergkamp (3)	G P Barber	7 / 0
27/8/97	Southampton v Crystal Palace	(0) 1 / (0) 0	Davies	J T Winter	5 / 0
27/8/97	Tottenham v Aston Villa	(1) 3 / (1) 2	Ferdinand (2), Fox / Yorke, Collymore	M A Riley	0 / 0
27/8/97	Wimbledon v Chelsea	(0) 0 / (0) 2	Di Matteo, Petrescu	M J Bodenham	5 / 0
30/8/97	Arsenal v Tottenham	(0) 0 / (0) 0		G S Willard	6 / 1
30/8/97	Aston Villa v Leeds	(0) 1 / (0) 0	Yorke	P Jones	0 / 0
30/8/97	Chelsea v Southampton	(4) 4 / (1) 2	Petrescu, Lebouef, Hughes, Wise / Davies, Monkou	A B Wilkie	4 / 1
30/8/97	Crystal Palace v Blackburn	(0) 1 / (2) 2	Dyer / Sutton, Gallacher	K W Burge	3 / 0
30/8/97	Derby v Barnsley	(1) 1 / (0) 0	Eranio (pen)	P A Durkin	5 / 0
30/8/97	Manchester United v Coventry	(1) 3 / (0) 0	Cole, Keane, Poborsky	G R Ashby	1 / 0
30/8/97	Sheffield Wednesday v Leicester	(0) 1 / (0) 0	Carbone (pen)	P E Alcock	4 / 0
30/8/97	West Ham v Wimbledon	(0) 3 / (0) 1	Hartson, Rieper, Berkovic / Ekoku	G Poli	2 / 0
1/9/97	Bolton v Everton	(0) 0 / (0) 0		S J Lodge	1 / 0
13/9/97	Arsenal v Bolton	(3) 4 / (1) 1	Wright (3), Parlour / Thompson	S W Dunn	7 / 0
13/9/97	Barnsley v Aston Villa	(0) 0 / (1) 3	Ehiogu, Draper, Taylor	G P Barber	1 / 0
13/9/97	Coventry v Southampton	(0) 1 / (0) 0	Soltvedt	U D Rennie	3 / 0
13/9/97	Crystal Palace v Chelsea	(0) 0 / (2) 3	M Hughes, Lebouef, Le Saux	G R Ashby	6 / 0
13/9/97	Derby v Everton	(2) 3 / (1) 1	Hunt, C Powell, Sturridge / Stuart	M A Riley	8 / 0
13/9/97	Leicester v Tottenham	(0) 3 / (0) 0	Walsh, Guppy, Heskey	A B Wilkie	1 / 0
13/9/97	Liverpool v Sheff Wednesday	(0) 2 / (0) 1	Ince, Thomas / Collins	G Poli	2 / 0
13/9/97	Manchester United v West Ham	(1) 2 / (1) 1	Keane, Scholes / Hartson	D R Elleray	3 / 0
13/9/97	Newcastle v Wimbledon	(1) 1 / (1) 3	Barton / Cort, Perry, Ekoku	M D Reed	3 / 0
14/9/97	Blackburn v Leeds	(3) 3 / (4) 4	Gallacher, Sutton (pen), Dahlin / Wallace (2), Molenaar, Hopkin	S W Dunn	7 / 0
20/9/97	Aston Villa v Derby	(0) 2 / (1) 1	Yorke, Joachim / Baiano	J T Winter	0 / 0
20/9/97	Bolton v Manchester United	(0) 0 / (0) 0		P A Durkin	6 / 2
20/9/97	Everton v Barnsley	(2) 4 / (1) 2	Speed (2, 1 pen), Cadamarteri, Oster / Redfearn, Barnard	G R Ashby	5 / 0
20/9/97	Leeds v Leicester	(0) 0 / (1) 1	Walsh	K W Burge	4 / 0
20/9/97	Sheffield Wednesday v Coventry	(0) 0 / (0) 0		G S Willard	3 / 0
20/9/97	Southampton v Liverpool	(0) 1 / (1) 1	Davies / Riedle	P Jones	3 / 0
20/9/97	Tottenham v Blackburn	(0) 0 / (0) 0		G P Barber	2 / 1
20/9/97	West Ham v Newcastle	(0) 0 / (1) 1	Barnes	S W Dunn	4 / 0
20/9/97	Wimbledon v Crystal Palace	(0) 0 / (0) 1	Lombardo	P E Alcock	4 / 0
21/9/97	Chelsea v Arsenal	(1) 2 / (1) 3	Poyet, Zoia / Bergkamp (2), Winterburn	D J Gallagher	4 / 1
22/9/97	Liverpool v Aston Villa	(0) 3 / (0) 0	Fowler (pen), McManaman, Riedle	M J Bodenham	3 / 0
23/9/97	Bolton v Tottenham	(1) 1 / (0) 1	Thompson (pen) / Armstrong	U D Rennie	5 / 0
23/9/97	Wimbledon v Barnsley	(0) 4 / (1) 1	Cort, Earle, Hughes, Ekoku / Tinkler	J T Winter	3 / 0
24/9/97	Arsenal v West Ham	(4) 4 / (0) 0	Bergkamp, Overmars (2), Wright (pen)	P E Alcock	4 / 0
24/9/97	Coventry v Crystal Palace	(1) 1 / (1) 1	Dublin / Fullarton	G P Barber	3 / 0
24/9/97	Leicester v Blackburn	(1) 1 / (1) 1	Izzet / Sutton	N S Barry	3 / 0
24/9/97	Manchester United v Chelsea	(1) 2 / (1) 2	Scholes, Solskjaer / Berg (og), M Hughes	G S Willard	8 / 0
24/9/97	Newcastle v Everton	(0) 1 / (0) 0	Lee	G Poli	2 / 1
24/9/97	Sheff Wednesday v Derby	(2) 2 / (3) 5	Di Canio, Carbone (pen) / Baiano (2), Laursen, Wanchope, Burton	M D Reed	2 / 1
24/9/97	Southampton v Leeds	(0) 0 / (1) 2	Molenaar, Wallace	S J Lodge	3 / 0
27/9/97	Aston Villa v Sheff Wednesday	(1) 2 / (2) 2	Staunton, Taylor / Collins, Whittingham	N S Barry	0 / 0

DATE	TEAMS & GAME	SCORES	GOAL SCORERS	REFEREE	CARDS
27/9/97	Barnsley v Leicester	(0) 0 / (0) 2	Marshall, Fenton	G Poll	6 / 0
27/9/97	Chelsea v Newcastle	(0) 1 / (0) 0	Poyet	M A Riley	1 / 0
27/9/97	Crystal Palace v Bolton	(2) 2 / (1) 2	Warhurst, Gordon / Beardsley, Johansen	D R Elleray	5 / 0
27/9/97	Derby v Southampton	(0) 4 / (0) 0	Eranio (pen), Wanchope, Baiano, Carsley	K W Burge	3 / 0
27/9/97	Everton v Arsenal	(0) 2 / (2) 2	Ball, Cadamarteri / Wright, Overmars	A B Wilkie	0 / 0
27/9/97	Leeds v Manchester United	(1) 1 / (0) 0	Wetherall	M J Bodenham	5 / 0
27/9/97	Tottenham v Wimbledon	(0) 0 / (0) 0		P A Durkin	0 / 0
27/9/97	West Ham v Liverpool	(1) 2 / (0) 1	Hartson, Berkovic / Fowler	D J Gallagher	2 / 0
28/9/97	Blackburn v Coventry	(0) 0 / (0) 0		P Jones	1 / 2
4/10/97	Arsenal v Barnsley	(3) 5 / (0) 0	Bergkamp (2), Parlour, Platt, Wright	P Jones	2 / 0
4/10/97	Bolton v Aston Villa	(0) 0 / (1) 1	Milosevic	G Poll	3 / 2
4/10/97	Coventry v Leeds	(0) 0 / (0) 0		A B Wilkie	4 / 0
4/10/97	Manchester United v Crystal Palace	(2) 2 / (0) 0	Sheringham, Hreidarsson (og)	S J Lodge	0 / 0
4/10/97	Newcastle v Tottenham	(0) 1 / (0) 0	Barton	M J Bodenham	1 / 0
4/10/97	Sheffield Wednesday v Everton	(0) 3 / (0) 1	Carbone (2, 1 pen), Di Canio / Cadamarteri	P A Durkin	3 / 0
4/10/97	Southampton v West Ham	(0) 3 / (0) 0	Ostenstad, Davies, Dodd	M A Riley	3 / 0
4/10/97	Wimbledon v Blackburn	(0) 0 / (1) 1	Sutton	D J Gallagher	0 / 0
5/10/97	Liverpool v Chelsea	(2) 4 / (1) 2	Berger (3), Fowler / Zola, Poyet (pen)	D R Elleray	4 / 1
6/10/97	Leicester v Derby	(0) 1 / (1) 2	Elliot / Baiano (2)	G R Ashby	3 / 0
18/10/97	Aston Villa v Wimbledon	(1) 1 / (1) 2	Taylor / Earle, Cort	K W Burge	1 / 0
18/10/97	Blackburn v Southampton	(1) 1 / (0) 0	Sherwood	G S Willard	1 / 0
18/10/97	Chelsea v Leicester	(0) 1 / (0) 0	Leboeuf	U D Rennie	2 / 0
18/10/97	Crystal Palace v Arsenal	(0) 0 / (0) 0		S W Dunn	5 / 0
18/10/97	Derby v Manchester United	(2) 2 / (0) 2	Baiano, Wanchope / Sheringham, Cole	G Poll	7 / 0
18/10/97	Everton v Liverpool	(1) 2 / (0) 0	Ruddock (og), Cadamarteri	M D Reed	6 / 0
18/10/97	Leeds v Newcastle	(3) 4 / (0) 1	Ribeiro, Kewell, Beresford (og), Wetherall / Gillespie	D R Elleray	6 / 0
18/10/97	West Ham v Bolton	(0) 3 / (0) 0	Berkovic, Hartson (2)	G R Ashby	7 / 1
19/10/97	Tottenham v Sheffield Wednesday	(3) 3 / (0) 2	Dominguez, Armstrong, Ginola / Collins, Di Canio	J T Winter	1 / 0
20/10/97	Barnsley v Coventry	(1) 2 / (0) 0	Ward, Redfearn (pen)	P E Alcock	6 / 0
22/10/97	Derby v Wimbledon	(0) 1 / (0) 1	Baiano / Rowett (og)	U D Rennie	3 / 0
25/10/97	Coventry v Everton	(0) 0 / (0) 0		S J Lodge	4 / 0
25/10/97	Liverpool v Derby	(1) 4 / (0) 0	Fowler (2), Leonhardsen, McManaman	G S Willard	3 / 0
25/10/97	Manchester United v Barnsley	(4) 7 / (0) 0	Cole (3), Giggs (2), Scholes, Poborsky	M A Riley	0 / 0
25/10/97	Newcastle v Blackburn	(1) 1 / (0) 1	Gillespie / Sutton	J T Winter	8 / 0
25/10/97	Sheffield Wednesday v Crystal Palace	(0) 1 / (1) 3	Collins / Hreidarsson, Rodger, Shipperley	D J Gallagher	0 / 0
25/10/97	Southampton v Tottenham	(0) 3 / (1) 2	Vega (og), Hirst (2) / Dominguez, Ginola	M S Barry	5 / 0
25/10/97	Wimbledon v Leeds	(1) 1 / (0) 0	Ardley (pen)	G P Barber	3 / 0
26/10/97	Arsenal v Aston Villa	(0) 0 / (0) 0		P A Durkin	4 / 0
26/10/97	Bolton v Chelsea	(0) 1 / (0) 0	Holdsworth	P Jones	2 / 0
27/10/97	Leicester v West Ham	(1) 2 / (0) 1	Heskey, Marshall / Berkovic	M D Reed	4 / 0
1/11/97	Aston Villa v Chelsea	(0) 0 / (1) 2	Hughes, Flo	S W Dunn	1 / 0
1/11/97	Barnsley v Blackburn	(0) 1 / (1) 1	Bosancic / Sherwood	G Poll	3 / 0
1/11/97	Bolton v Liverpool	(0) 1 / (1) 1	Blake / Fowler	D J Gallacher	4 / 1
1/11/97	Derby v Arsenal	(0) 3 / (0) 0	Wanchope (2), Sturridge	P E Alcock	5 / 0
1/11/97	Manchester United v Sheffield Wednesday	(4) 6 / (0) 1	Sheringham (2), Cole (2), Solskjaer (2) / Whittingham	G R Ashby	1 / 0
1/11/97	Newcastle v Leicester	(2) 3 / (2) 3	Barnes (pen), Tomasson, Beresford / Marshall (2), Elliot	G S Willard	4 / 1
1/11/97	Tottenham v Leeds	(0) 0 / (1) 1	Wallace	K W Burge	3 / 0
1/11/97	Wimbledon v Coventry	(1) 1 / (2) 2	Cort / Huckerby, Dublin	U D Rennie	3 / 0
2/11/97	Everton v Southampton	(0) 0 / (1) 2	Le Tissier, Davies	A B Wilkie	3 / 0
8/11/97	Blackburn v Everton	(1) 3 / (1) 2	Gallacher, Duff, Sherwood / Speed, Ferguson	P E Alcock	3 / 0
8/11/97	Coventry v Newcastle	(1) 2 / (1) 2	Dublin (2) / Barnes, Lee	P A Durkin	3 / 0
8/11/97	Crystal Palace v Aston Villa	(1) 1 / (0) 1	Shipperley / Joachim	J T Winter	4 / 1
8/11/97	Leeds v Derby	(2) 4 / (3) 3	Wallace, Kewell, Hasselbaink (pen), Bowyer / Sturridge (2), Asanovic (pen)	N S Barry	4 / 0
8/11/97	Liverpool v Tottenham	(0) 4 / (0) 0	McManaman, Leonhardsen, Redknapp, Owen	S J Lodge	1 / 0
8/11/97	Sheffield Wednesday v Bolton	(5) 5 / (0) 0	Di Canio, Whittingham, Booth (3)	M D Reed	7 / 0
8/11/97	Southampton v Barnsley	(3) 4 / (1) 1	Le Tissier (pen), Palmer, Davies, Hirst / Bosancic (pen)	G R Ashby	6 / 0
9/11/97	Arsenal v Manchester United	(2) 3 / (2) 2	Anelka, Viera, Platt / Sheringham (2)	M J Bodenham	4 / 0
9/11/97	Chelsea v West Ham	(0) 2 / (0) 1	Ferdinand (og), Zola / Hartson (pen)	G P Barber	5 / 0
10/11/97	Leicester v Wimbledon	(0) 0 / (0) 1	Gayle	M A Riley	2 / 0
22/11/97	Aston Villa v Everton	(1) 2 / (0) 1	Milosevic, Ehiogu / Speed (pen)	U D Rennie	4 / 0
22/11/97	Blackburn v Chelsea	(1) 1 / (0) 0	Croft	S J lodge	4 / 0
22/11/97	Derby v Coventry	(3) 3 / (0) 1	Baiano, Eranio (pen), Wanchope / Huckerby	D R Elleray	9 / 0
22/11/97	Leicester v Bolton	(0) 0 / (0) 0		G P Barber	3 / 0
22/11/97	Liverpool v Barnsley	(0) 0 / (1) 1	Ward	J T Winter	1 / 0
22/11/97	Newcastle v Southampton	(0) 2 / (1) 1	Barnes (2) / Davies	D J Gallagher	3 / 0
22/11/97	Sheffield Wednesday v Arsenal	(1) 2 / (0) 0	Booth, Whittingham	K W Burge	5 / 0
22/11/97	Wimbledon v Manchester United	(0) 2 / (0) 5	Ardley, M Hughes / Butt, Beckham (2), Scholes, Cole	P A Durkin	3 / 0
23/11/97	Leeds v West Ham	(0) 3 / (0) 1	Hasselbaink (2), Haaland / Lampard	G R Ashby	1 / 0
24/11/97	Tottenham v Crystal Palace	(0) 0 / (0) 1	Shipperley	P A Durkin	2 / 0
26/11/97	Chelsea v Everton	(0) 2 / (0) 0	Wise (pen), Zola (pen)	N S Barry	4 / 1
29/11/97	Barnsley v Leeds	(2) 2 / (1) 3	Liddell, Ward / Haaland, Wallace, Lilley	M D Reed	9 / 0
29/11/97	Bolton v Wimbledon	(0) 1 / (0) 0	Blake	J T Winter	1 / 0
29/11/97	Chelsea v Derby	(2) 4 / (0) 0	Zola (3), M Hughes	U D Rennie	5 / 0
29/11/97	Coventry v Leicester	(0) 0 / (1) 2	Fenton, Elliot (pen)	M J Bodenham	3 / 0
29/11/97	Crystal Palace v Newcastle	(0) 1 / (1) 2	Shipperley / Ketsbaia, Tomasson	M A Riley	4 / 0
29/11/97	Everton v Tottenham	(0) 0 / (0) 2	Vega, Ginola	P Jones	3 / 0

DATE	TEAMS & GAME	SCORES	GOAL SCORERS	REFEREE	CARDS
29/11/97	Southampton v Sheffield Wednesday	(0) 2 (1) 3	Hirst, Palmer Atherton, Collins, Di Canio	S W Dunn	1 0
29/11/97	West Ham v Aston Villa	(1) 2 (0) 1	Hartson (2) Yorke	P E Alcock	1 0
30/11/97	Arsenal v Liverpool	(0) 0 (0) 1	 McManaman	G Poll	4 0
30/11/97	Manchester United v Blackburn	(1) 4 (0) 0	Solskjaer (2), Henchoz (og), Kenna (og)	A B Wilkie	1 1
1/12/97	Bolton v Newcastle	(1) 1 (0) 0	Blake	N S Barry	3 0
3/12/97	West Ham v Crystal Palace	(2) 4 (1) 1	Hartson, Berkovic, Unsworth, Lomas Shipperley	D R Elleray	1 0
6/12/97	Aston Villa v Coventry	(1) 3 (0) 0	Collymore, Hendrie, Joachim	G P Barber	5 2
6/12/97	Blackburn v Bolton	(2) 3 (0) 1	Gallacher, Sutton, Wilcox Frandsen	M A Riley	6 1
6/12/97	Derby v West Ham	(1) 2 (0) 0	Sturridge (2)	A B Wilkie	5 0
6/12/97	Leeds v Everton	(0) 0 (0) 0		P A Durkin	4 0
6/12/97	Leicester v Crystal Palace	(0) 1 (1) 1	Izzet Padovano	U D Rennie	4 1
6/12/97	Liverpool v Manchester United	(0) 1 (0) 3	Fowler (pen) Cole (2), Beckham	D R Elleray	4 0
6/12/97	Newcastle v Arsenal	(0) 0 (1) 1	 Wright	S W Dunn	2 0
6/12/97	Tottenham v Chelsea	(1) 1 (1) 6	Vega Flo (3), Di Matteo, Petrescu, Nicholls,	D J Gallagher	1 0
7/12/97	Wimbledon v Southampton	(1) 1 (0) 0	Earle	M D Reed	1 0
8/12/97	Sheffield Wednesday v Barnsley	(1) 2 (1) 1	Stefanovic, Di Canio Redfearn	G S Willard	2 0
13/12/97	Arsenal v Blackburn	(1) 1 (0) 3	Overmars Wilcox, Gallacher, Sherwood	G S Willard	8 0
13/12/97	Barnsley v Newcastle	(1) 2 (1) 2	Redfearn, Hendrie Gillespie (2)	P E Alcock	5 0
13/12/97	Chelsea v Leeds	(0) 0 (0) 0		G Poll	6 2
13/12/97	Coventry v Tottenham	(1) 4 (0) 0	Huckerby (2), Breen, Hall	S W Dunn	1 0
13/12/97	Crystal Palace v Liverpool	(0) 0 (1) 3	 McManaman, Owen, Leonhardsen	N S Barry	2 0
13/12/97	Everton v Wimbledon	(0) 0 (0) 0		G R Ashby	0 0
13/12/97	Southampton v Leicester	(1) 2 (0) 1	Le Tissier, Benali Savage	S J Lodge	2 0
13/12/97	West Ham v Sheffield Wednesday	(0) 1 (0) 0	Kitson	M A Riley	2 0
14/12/97	Bolton v Derby	(0) 3 (0) 3	Thompson (pen), Blake, Pollock Eranio, Baiano (2)	U D Rennie	3 0
15/12/97	Manchester United v Aston Villa	(0) 1 (0) 0	Giggs	P A Durkin	3 0
17/12/97	Newcastle v Derby	(0) 0 (0) 0		K W Burge	4 1
20/12/97	Aston Villa v Southampton	(0) 1 (0) 1	Taylor Ostenstad	D R Elleray	0 0
20/12/97	Blackburn v West Ham	(1) 3 (0) 0	Ripley, Duff (2)	G R Ashby	1 1
20/12/97	Derby v Crystal Palace	(0) 0 (0) 0		M J Bodenham	1 0
20/12/97	Leeds v Bolton	(0) 2 (0) 0	Ribeiro, Hasselbaink	A B Wilkie	8 0
20/12/97	Leicester v Everton	(0) 0 (0) 1	 Speed (pen)	J T Winter	7 0
20/12/97	Liverpool v Coventry	(1) 1 (0) 0	Owen	P E Alcock	4 0
20/12/97	Sheffield Wednesday v Chelsea	(0) 1 (1) 4	Pembridge Petrescu, Vialli, Leboeuf (pen), Flo	G P Barber	1 0
20/12/97	Tottenham v Barnsley	(3) 3 (0) 0	Neilsen, Ginola (2)	M D Reed	5 0
21/12/97	Newcastle v Manchester United	(0) 0 (0) 1	 Cole	P Jones	7 0
26/12/97	Arsenal v Leicester	(1) 2 (0) 1	Platt, Walsh (og) Lennon	D R Elleray	3 0
26/12/97	Aston Villa v Tottenham	(1) 4 (0) 1	Draper (2), Collymore (2) Calderwood	A B Wilkie	1 0
26/12/97	Bolton Barnsley	(1) 1 (1) 1	Bergsson Hristov	S W Dunn	3 0
26/12/97	Chelsea v Wimbledon	(1) 1 (1) 1	Vialli Hughes	G S Willard	3 0
26/12/97	Crystal Palace v Southampton	(0) 1 (1) 1	Shipperley Oakley	P E Alcock	4 0
26/12/97	Derby v Newcastle	(1) 1 (0) 0	Eranio (pen)	M D Reed	6 1
26/12/97	Liverpool v Leeds	(0) 3 (0) 1	Owen, Fowler (2) Haaland	S J Lodge	1 0
26/12/97	Manchester United v Everton	(2) 2 (0) 0	Berg, Cole	U D Rennie	5 0
26/12/97	Sheffield Wednesday v Blackburn	(0) 0 (0) 0		J T Winter	1 0
26/12/97	West Ham v Coventry	(1) 1 (0) 0	Kitson	G Poll	4 1
28/12/97	Barnsley v Derby	(0) 1 (0) 0	Ward	G P Barber	5 0
28/12/97	Blackburn v Crystal Palace	(1) 2 (1) 2	Gallacher, Sutton Dyer, Warhurst	P Jones	1 0
28/12/97	Coventry v Manchester United	(1) 3 (1) 2	Whelan, Dublin (pen), Huckerby Solskjaer, Sheringham	N S Barry	2 0
28/12/97	Everton v Bolton	(2) 3 (2) 2	Ferguson (3) Bergsson, Sellars	K W Burge	2 0
28/12/97	Leeds v Aston Villa	(0) 1 (0) 1	Hasselbaink Milosevic	D J Gallagher	3 0
28/12/97	Leicester v Sheffield Wednesday	(1) 1 (0) 1	Guppy Booth	G Poll	5 1
28/12/97	Newcastle v Liverpool	(1) 1 (2) 2	Watson McManaman (2)	G R Ashby	1 0
28/12/97	Tottenham v Arsenal	(1) 1 (0) 1	Neilsen Parlour	M A Riley	4 0
28/12/97	Wimbledon v West Ham	(0) 1 (1) 2	Solbakken Kimble (og), Kitson	P A Durkin	0 1
29/12/97	Southampton v Chelsea	(1) 1 (0) 0	Davies	M J Bodenham	1 0
10/1/98	Arsenal v Leeds	(0) 2 (0) 1	Overmars (2) Hasselbaink	G R Ashby	2 0
10/1/98	Aston Villa v Leicester	(0) 1 (0) 1	Joachim Parker (pen)	M A Riley	3 0
10/1/98	Bolton v Southampton	(0) 0 (0) 0		G S Willard	3 1
10/1/98	Chelsea v Coventry	(0) 3 (1) 1	Nicholls (2), Di Matteo Telfer	M D Reed	5 0
10/1/98	Crystal Palace v Everton	(1) 1 (3) 3	Dyer (pen) Barmby, Ferguson, Madar	G P Barber	3 0
10/1/98	Liverpool v Wimbledon	(0) 2 (0) 0	Redknapp (2)	M J Bodenham	2 0
10/1/98	Manchester United v Tottenham	(1) 2 (0) 0	Giggs (2)	P E Alcock	1 0
10/1/98	Sheffield Wednesday v Newcastle	(1) 2 (1) 1	Di Canio, Newsome Tomasson	D R Elleray	5 0
10/1/98	West Ham v Barnsley	(2) 6 (0) 0	Lampard, Abou (2), Moncur, Hartson, Lazaridis	N S Barry	2 0
11/1/98	Derby v Blackburn	(2) 3 (0) 1	Sturridge (2), Wanchope Sutton	G Poll	3 0
17/1/98	Barnsley v Crystal Palace	(1) 1 (0) 0	Ward	M D Reed	7 0
17/1/98	Blackburn v Aston Villa	(2) 5 (0) 0	Sherwood, Gallacher (3), Ripley	K W Burge	2 0
17/1/98	Coventry v Arsenal	(1) 2 (0) 2	Whelan, Dublin (pen) Bergkamp, Anelka	S J Lodge	4 2
17/1/98	Leeds v Sheffield Wednesday	(0) 1 (0) 2	Pembridge (og) Newsome, Booth	M J Bodenham	2 0
17/1/98	Leicester v Liverpool	(0) 0 (0) 0		S W Dunn	2 0
17/1/98	Newcastle v Bolton	(1) 2 (0) 1	Barnes, Ketsbaia Blake	G Poll	3 0
17/1/98	Tottenham v West Ham	(1) 1 (0) 0	Klinsmann	D R Elleray	4 1
17/1/98	Wimbledon v Derby	(0) 0 (0) 0		P Jones	4 0
18/1/98	Everton v Chelsea	(1) 3 (1) 1	Speed, Ferguson, Duberry (og) Flo	A B Wilkie	3 0
19/1/98	Southampton v Manchester United	(1) 1 (0) 0	Davies	M A Riley	5 0

Every game

DATE	TEAMS & GAME	SCORES	GOAL SCORERS	REFEREE	CARDS
20/1/98	Liverpool v Newcastle	(1) 1 / (0) 0	Owen	G P Barber	4 / 0
31/1/98	Arsenal v Southampton	(0) 3 / (0) 0	Bergkamp, Adams, Anelka	P Jones	6 / 0
31/1/98	Bolton v Coventry	(1) 1 / (1) 5	Sellars / Whelan, Huckerby (2), Dublin (2)	D J Gallagher	3 / 0
31/1/98	Chelsea v Barnsley	(1) 2 / (0) 0	Vialli, Hughes	J T Winter	7 / 0
31/1/98	Crystal Palace v Leeds	(0) 0 / (2) 2	Wallace, Hasselbaink	U D Rennie	4 / 0
31/1/98	Derby v Tottenham	(1) 2 / (0) 1	Sturridge, Wanchope / Fox	G S Willard	5 / 0
31/1/98	Liverpool v Blackburn	(0) 0 / (0) 0		P A Durkin	1 / 0
31/1/98	Manchester United v Leicester	(0) 0 / (1) 1	Cottee	G R Ashby	3 / 0
31/1/98	Sheffield Wednesday v Wimbledon	(1) 1 / (1) 1	Pembridge / Hughes	A B Wilkie	4 / 0
31/1/98	West Ham v Everton	(1) 2 / (1) 2	Sinclair (2) / Barmby, Madar	M D Reed	2 / 0
1/2/98	Aston Villa v Newcastle	(0) 0 / (0) 1	Batty	S J Lodge	0 / 0
7/2/98	Barnsley v Everton	(1) 2 / (1) 2	Fjortoft, Barnard / Ferguson, Grant	M J Bodenham	1 / 0
7/2/98	Blackburn v Tottenham	(0) 0 / (1) 3	Berti, Armstrong, Fox	G P Barber	4 / 0
7/2/98	Coventry v Sheffield Wednesday	(0) 1 / (0) 0	Dublin (pen)	G R Ashby	0 / 0
7/2/98	Derby v Aston Villa	(0) 0 / (0) 1	Yorke	P E Alcock	2 / 0
7/2/98	Leicester v Leeds	(1) 1 / (0) 0	Parker (pen)	N S Barry	7 / 0
7/2/98	Liverpool v Southampton	(1) 2 / (1) 3	Owen (2) / Hirst (2, 1 pen), Ostenstad	J T Winter	4 / 0
7/2/98	Manchester United v Bolton	(0) 1 / (0) 0	Cole / Taylor	S J Lodge	6 / 0
7/2/98	Newcastle v West Ham	(0) 0 / (0) 1	Lazaridis	U D Rennie	3 / 0
8/2/98	Arsenal v Chelsea	(2) 2 / (0) 0	Hughes (2)	D J Gallagher	7 / 0
9/2/98	Crystal Palace v Wimbledon	(0) 0 / (0) 3	Leaburn (2), Euell	K W Burge	2 / 0
14/2/98	Everton v Derby	(0) 1 / (1) 2	Thomsen / Stimac, Wanchope	S W Dunn	3 / 1
14/2/98	Sheffield Wednesday v Liverpool	(1) 3 / (1) 3	Carbone, Di Canio, Hinchcliffe / Owen (3)	M D Reed	3 / 0
14/2/98	Tottenham v Leicester	(1) 1 / (1) 1	Calderwood / Cottee	S J Lodge	2 / 0
18/2/98	Aston Villa v Manchester United	(0) 0 / (0) 2	Beckham, Giggs	M J Bodenham	2 / 0
18/2/98	Southampton v Coventry	(0) 1 / (2) 2	Le Tissier (pen) / Whelan, Huckerby	P E Alcock	0 / 0
21/2/98	Arsenal v Crystal Palace	(1) 1 / (0) 0	Grimandi	J T Winter	7 / 0
21/2/98	Bolton v West Ham	(0) 1 / (0) 1	Blake / Sinclair	P E Alcock	0 / 1
21/2/98	Coventry v Barnsley	(0) 1 / (0) 0	Dublin (pen)	A B Wilkie	2 / 0
21/2/98	Leicester v Chelsea	(1) 2 / (0) 0	Heskey (2)	P A Durkin	5 / 0
21/2/98	Manchester United v Derby	(1) 2 / (0) 0	Giggs, Irwin (pen)	M D Reed	1 / 0
21/2/98	Sheffield Wednesday v Tottenham	(1) 1 / (0) 0	Di Canio	M J Bodenham	5 / 0
21/2/98	Southampton v Blackburn	(1) 3 / (0) 0	Ostenstad (2), Hirst	M D Reed	1 / 0
21/2/98	Wimbledon v Aston Villa	(2) 2 / (1) 1	Euell, Leaburn / Milosevic	G R Ashby	3 / 0
22/2/98	Newcastle v Leeds	(0) 1 / (0) 1	Ketsbaia / Wallace	G S Willard	6 / 0
23/2/98	Liverpool v Everton	(0) 1 / (0) 1	Ince / Ferguson	P Jones	3 / 0
28/2/98	Aston Villa v Liverpool	(1) 2 / (1) 1	Collymore (2) / Owen (pen)	G Poll	5 / 0
28/2/98	Barnsley v Wimbledon	(1) 2 / (0) 1	Fjortoft (2) / Euell	G P Barber	5 / 0

DATE	TEAMS & GAME	SCORES	GOAL SCORERS	REFEREE	CARDS
28/2/98	Blackburn Rovers v Leicester City	(3) 5 / (0) 3	Dahlin, Sutton (3), Hendry / Wilson, Izzet, Ullathorne	N S Barry	3 / 0
28/2/98	Chelsea v Manchester United	(0) 0 / (1) 1	P Neville	S W Dunn	6 / 0
28/2/98	Crystal Palace v Coventry City	(0) 0 / (2) 3	Telfer, Moldovan, Dublin	D R Elleray	4 / 0
28/2/98	Derby County v Sheffield Wednesday	(1) 3 / (0) 0	Wanchope (2), Rowett	A B Wilkie	3 / 0
28/2/98	Everton v Newcastle United	(0) 0 / (0) 0		M A Riley	1 / 0
28/2/98	Leeds United v Southampton	(0) 0 / (0) 1	Hirst	K W Burge	1 / 1
1/3/98	Tottenham v Bolton	(1) 1 / (0) 0	Nielsen	P Jones	4 / 0
2/3/98	West Ham v Arsenal	(0) 0 / (0) 0		P A Durkin	1 / 0
4/3/98	Leeds v Tottenham	(1) 1 / (0) 0	Kewell	P E Alcock	2 / 0
7/3/98	Liverpool v Bolton	(0) 2 / (1) 1	Ince, Owen / Thompson	K W Burge	2 / 0
7/3/98	Sheffield Wednesday v Manchester United	(1) 2 / (0) 0	Atherton, Di Canio	P Jones	2 / 0
7/3/98	Southampton v Everton	(0) 2 / (0) 1	Le Tissier (pen), Ostenstad / Tiler	D R Elleray	3 / 2
8/3/98	Chelsea v Aston Villa	(0) 0 / (0) 1	Joachim	S J Lodge	2 / 0
11/3/98	Aston Villa v Barnsley	(0) 0 / (0) 1	Ward	P Jones	0 / 0
11/3/98	Chelsea v Crystal Palace	(3) 6 / (1) 2	Vialli (2), Zola, Wise, Flo (2) / Hreidarsson, Bent	M A Riley	3 / 0
11/3/98	Leeds v Blackburn	(0) 4 / (0) 0	Bowyer, Hasselbaink, Haaland (2)	D R Elleray	1 / 0
11/3/98	West Ham v Manchester United	(1) 1 / (0) 1	Sinclair / Scholes	G S Willard	3 / 0
11/3/98	Wimbledon v Arsenal	(0) 0 / (1) 1	Wreh	D J Gallagher	1 / 0
14/3/98	Aston Villa v Crystal Palace	(3) 3 / (0) 1	Taylor, Milosevic (2, 1 pen) / Jansen	G P Barber	3 / 0
14/3/98	Barnsley v Southampton	(3) 4 / (2) 3	Ward, Jones, Fjortoft, Redfearn (pen) / Ostenstad , Le Tissier (2)	G R Ashby	1 / 0
14/3/98	Bolton v Sheffield Wednesday	(1) 3 / (1) 2	Frandsen, Blake, Thompson (pen) / Booth, Atherton	G Poll	3 / 0
14/3/98	Everton v Blackburn	(0) 1 / (0) 0	Madar	G S Willard	7 / 0
14/3/98	Manchester United v Arsenal	(0) 0 / (0) 1	Overmars	A B Wilkie	5 / 0
14/3/98	Newcastle v Coventry	(0) 0 / (0) 0		P Jones	2 / 0
14/3/98	Tottenham v Liverpool	(1) 3 / (1) 3	Klinsmann, Ginola, Vega / McManaman (2), Ince	U D Rennie	5 / 0
14/3/98	West Ham v Manchester United	(0) 2 / (0) 1	Sinclair, Unsworth / Charvet	M J Bodenham	3 / 0
14/3/98	Wimbledon v Leicester	(0) 2 / (0) 1	Roberts, M Hughes / Savage	M A Riley	3 / 0
15/3/98	Derby v Leeds	(0) 0 / (3) 5	Laursen (og), Halle, Bowyer, Kewell, Hasselbaink	S J Lodge	3 / 0
18/3/98	Newcastle v Crystal Palace	(0) 1 / (2) 2	Shearer / Lombardo, Jansen	S J Lodge	6 / 0
28/3/98	Arsenal v Sheffield Wednesday	(1) 1 / (0) 0	Bergkamp	S W Dunn	2 / 0
28/3/98	Barnsley v Liverpool	(1) 2 / (1) 3	Redfearn (2, 1 pen) / Riedle (2), McManaman	G S Willard	3 / 3
28/3/98	Bolton v Leicester	(0) 2 / (0) 0	Thompson (2)	U D Rennie	4 / 2
28/3/98	Coventry v Derby	(0) 1 / (0) 0	Huckerby	K W Burge	1 / 0
28/3/98	Crystal Palace v Tottenham	(0) 1 / (0) 3	Shipperley / Berti, Armstrong, Klinsmann	M D Reed	4 / 0
28/3/98	Everton v Aston Villa	(1) 1 / (0) 4	Madar / Joachim, Charles, Yorke (2, 1 pen)	N S Barry	6 / 0
28/3/98	Manchester United v Wimbledon	(0) 2 / (0) 0	Johnsen, Scholes	D J Gallagher	4 / 0
28/3/98	Southampton v Newcastle	(0) 2 / (0) 1	Pearce (og), Le Tissier (pen) / Lee	G P Barber	5 / 0
30/3/98	West Ham v Leeds	(2) 3 / (0) 0	Hartson, Abou, Pearce	A B Wilkie	6 / 0

DATE	TEAMS & GAME	SCORES	GOAL SCORERS	REFEREE	CARDS
31/3/98	Blackburn v Barnsley	(1) 2 / (0) 1	Dahlin, Gallacher / Hristov	M D Reed	5 / 0
31/3/98	Bolton v Arsenal	(0) 0 / (0) 1	Wreh	K W Burge	2 / 1
31/3/98	Wimbledon v Newcastle	(0) 0 / (0) 0		N S Barry	0 / 0
4/4/98	Aston Villa v West Ham	(0) 2 / (0) 0	Joachim, Milosevic	S W Dunn	0 / 0
4/4/98	Leeds v Barnsley	(1) 2 / (1) 1	Hasselbaink, Moses (og) / Hristov	K W Burge	1 / 1
4/4/98	Leicester v Coventry	(0) 1 / (0) 1	Wilson / Whelan	G P Barber	3 / 0
4/4/98	Sheffield Wednesday v Southampton	(0) 1 / (0) 0	Carbone	P Jones	1 / 0
4/4/98	Tottenham v Everton	(0) 1 / (1) 1	Armstrong / Madar	A B Wilkie	8 / 0
4/4/98	Wimbledon v Bolton	(0) 0 / (0) 0		M J Bodenham	0 / 0
5/4/98	Derby v Chelsea	(0) 0 / (1) 1	M Hughes	J T Winter	1 / 0
6/4/98	Blackburn v Manchester United	(1) 1 / (0) 3	Sutton (pen) / Cole, Scholes, Beckham	G R Ashby	5 / 0
8/4/98	Leeds v Chelsea	(2) 3 / (1) 1	Hasselbaink (2), Wetherall / Charvet	D R Elleray	3 / 0
10/4/98	Manchester United v Liverpool	(1) 1 / (1) 1	Johnsen / Owen	G Poll	2 / 1
11/4/98	Arsenal v Newcastle	(1) 3 / (0) 1	Anelka (2), Vieira / Barton	G S Willard	2 / 0
11/4/98	Barnsley v Sheffield Wednesday	(0) 2 / (0) 1	Ward, Fjortoft / Stefanovic	P E Alcock	6 / 0
11/4/98	Bolton v Blackburn	(1) 2 / (0) 1	Holdsworth, Taylor / Duff	M A Riley	2 / 1
11/4/98	Chelsea v Tottenham	(0) 2 / (0) 0	Flo, Vialli	P A Durkin	1 / 0
11/4/98	Coventry v Aston Villa	(0) 1 / (1) 2	Whelan / Yorke (2)	D J Gallagher	2 / 0
11/4/98	Crystal Palace v Leicester	(0) 0 / (1) 3	Heskey (2), Elliot	A B Wilkie	1 / 0
11/4/98	Everton v Leeds	(2) 2 / (0) 0	Hutchison, Ferguson	U D Rennie	5 / 1
11/4/98	Southampton v Wimbledon	(0) 0 / (1) 1	Leaburn	M D Reed	1 / 0
11/4/98	West Ham v Derby	(0) 0 / (0) 0		G P Barber	7 / 2
13/4/98	Blackburn v Arsenal	(0) 1 / (4) 4	Gallacher / Bergkamp, Parlour (2), Anelka	M J Bodenham	3 / 0
13/4/98	Derby v Bolton	(4) 4 / (0) 0	Wanchope, Burton (2), Baiano	D J Gallagher	2 / 0
13/4/98	Liverpool v Crystal Palace	(1) 2 / (0) 1	Leonhardsen, Thompson / Bent	G P Barber	2 / 0
13/4/98	Newcastle v Barnsley	(1) 2 / (0) 1	Andersson, Shearer / Fjortoft	S W Dunn	6 / 0
13/4/98	Sheffield Wednesday v West Ham	(0) 1 / (1) 1	Magilton / Berkovic	N S Barry	2 / 0
13/4/98	Tottenham v Coventry	(0) 1 / (0) 1	Berti / Dublin	M A Riley	5 / 0
13/4/98	Wimbledon v Everton	(0) 0 / (0) 0		K W Burge	1 / 0
14/4/98	Leicester v Southampton	(1) 3 / (2) 3	Lennon, Elliot, Parker (pen) / Ostenstad, Hirst	G Poll	2 / 0
18/4/98	Arsenal v Wimbledon	(3) 5 / (0) 0	Adams, Overmars, Bergkamp, Petit, Wreh	P Jones	1 / 0
18/4/98	Barnsley v Tottenham	(1) 1 / (0) 1	Redfearn / Calderwood	M J Bodenham	5 / 1
18/4/98	Bolton v Leeds	(0) 2 / (2) 3	Thompson, Fish / Haaland, Halle, Hasselbaink	J T Winter	5 / 0
18/4/98	Crystal Palace v Derby	(0) 3 / (0) 1	Jansen, Curcic, Bent / Bohinen	P E Alcock	1 / 0
18/4/98	Everton v Leicester	(1) 1 / (1) 1	Madar / Marshall	S J Lodge	3 / 0
18/4/98	Manchester United v Newcastle	(1) 1 / (1) 1	Beckham / Andersson	U D Rennie	5 / 1
18/4/98	Southampton v Aston Villa	(1) 1 / (1) 2	Le Tissier / Hendrie, Yorke	A B Wilkie	0 / 0
18/4/98	West Ham v Blackburn	(2) 2 / (1) 1	Hartson (2) / Wilcox	P A Durkin	3 / 0
19/4/98	Chelsea v Sheffield Wednesday	(1) 1 / (0) 0	Leboeuf (pen)	G S Willard	3 / 0
19/4/98	Coventry v Liverpool	(0) 1 / (1) 1	Dublin (pen) / Owen	N S Barry	2 / 0
25/4/98	Aston Villa v Bolton	(0) 1 / (2) 3	Taylor / Cox, Taylor, Blake	D R Elleray	1 / 0
25/4/98	Barnsley v Arsenal	(0) 0 / (1) 2	Bergkamp, Overmars	M A Riley	3 / 0
25/4/98	Blackburn v Wimbledon	(0) 0 / (0) 0		G Poll	1 / 0
25/4/98	Chelsea v Liverpool	(1) 4 / (1) 1	M Hughes (2), Clarke, Flo / Riedle	G R Ashby	2 / 0
25/4/98	Everton v Sheffield Wednesday	(0) 1 / (2) 3	Ferguson / Pembridge, Di Canio	G P Barber	5 / 1
25/4/98	Leeds v Coventry	(2) 3 / (2) 3	Hasselbaink, Kewell / Huckerby (3)	M D Reed	6 / 0
25/4/98	Tottenham v Newcastle	(1) 2 / (0) 0	Klinsmann, Ferdinand	J T Winter	4 / 0
25/4/98	West Ham v Southampton	(1) 2 / (1) 4	Sinclair, Lomas / Le Tissier, Ostenstad (2), Palmer	D J Gallagher	1 / 0
26/4/98	Derby v Leicester	(0) 0 / (4) 4	Heskey (2), Izzet, Marshall	G S Willard	2 / 0
27/4/98	Crystal Palace v Manchester United	(0) 0 / (2) 3	Scholes, Butt, Cole	P Jones	1 / 0
29/4/98	Arsenal v Derby	(1) 1 / (0) 0	Petit	N S Barry	6 / 0
29/4/98	Chelsea v Blackburn	(0) 0 / (0) 1	Gallacher	P E Alcock	0 / 0
29/4/98	Coventry v Wimbledon	(0) 0 / (0) 0		J T Winter	2 / 0
29/4/98	Leicester v Newcastle	(0) 0 / (0) 0		M J Bodenham	4 / 0
2/5/98	Bolton v Crystal Palace	(3) 5 / (2) 2	Blake, Fish, Phillips, Thompson, Holdsworth / Gordon, Bent	N S Barry	5 / 1
2/5/98	Coventry v Blackburn	(2) 2 / (0) 0	Dublin (pen), Boateng	S J Lodge	2 / 1
2/5/98	Leicester v Barnsley	(0) 1 / (0) 0	Zagorakis	D J Gallagher	2 / 1
2/5/98	Liverpool v West Ham	(4) 5 / (0) 0	Owen, McAteer (2), Leonhardsen, Ince	J T Winter	6 / 0
2/5/98	Newcastle v Chelsea	(2) 3 / (0) 1	Dabizas, Lee, Speed / Di Matteo	K W Burge	3 / 0
2/5/98	Sheffield Wednesday v Aston Villa	(0) 1 / (2) 3	Sanetti / Yorke, Hendrie, Joachim	M J Bodenham	2 / 0
2/5/98	Southampton v Derby	(0) 0 / (0) 2	Dailly, Sturridge	M A Riley	6 / 1
2/5/98	Wimbledon v Tottenham	(2) 2 / (2) 6	Fear (2) / Ferdinand, Klinsmann (4), Saib	G P Barber	2 / 1
3/5/98	Arsenal v Everton	(2) 4 / (0) 0	Bilic (og), Overmars (2), Adams	G R Ashby	6 / 0
4/5/98	Manchester United v Leeds	(2) 3 / (0) 0	Giggs, Irwin (pen), Beckham	G Willard	5 / 1
5/5/98	Crystal Palace v West Ham	(1) 3 / (1) 3	Bent, Rodger, Lombardo / Curcic (og), Omoyinmi (2)	G Poll	3 / 1
6/5/98	Liverpool v Arsenal	(3) 4 / (0) 0	Ince (2), Owen, Leonhardsen	A B Wilkie	0 / 0
10/5/98	Aston Villa v Arsenal	(1) 1 / (0) 0	Yorke (pen)	G Poll	4 / 1
10/5/98	Barnsley v Manchester United	(0) 0 / (1) 2	Cole, Sheringham	P A Durkin	2 / 0
10/5/98	Blackburn v Newcastle	(0) 1 / (0) 0	Sutton	D Elleray	3 / 1
10/5/98	Chelsea v Bolton	(0) 2 / (0) 0	Vialli, Morris	A B Wilkie	4 / 0
10/5/98	Crystal Palace v Sheffield Wednesday	(0) 1 / (0) 0	Morrison	M D Reed	4 / 0
10/5/98	Derby v Liverpool	(0) 1 / (0) 0	Wanchope	S J Lodge	3 / 0
10/5/98	Everton v Coventry	(1) 1 / (0) 1	Farrelly / Dublin	P A Alcock	3 / 0
10/5/98	Leeds v Wimbledon	(0) 1 / (0) 0	Haaland / Ekoku	S W Dunn	0 / 0
10/5/98	Tottenham v Southampton	(1) 1 / (1) 1	Klinsmann / Le Tissier	P Jones	2 / 0
10/5/98	West Ham v Leicester	(2) 4 / (0) 3	Lampard, Abou (2), Sinclair / Cottee (2), Heskey	U D Rennie	4 / 0

August

Premiership 1997

Soaring temperatures see Manchester United and Blackburn Rovers set the pace with some scintillating football. And West Ham are up there too amongst the usual London suspects

The new Premiership season starts in the intense heat of high August and without its greatest star, Alan Shearer. The England captain injures his right ankle when his studs catch in the summer grass of Goodison Park while trying to stretch for the ball in the Umbro Tournament match against Chelsea on the last Saturday of July. "One thought kept running through my mind," Shearer said. "What a stupid way to get injured." He will be out of action until the New Year.

Champions Manchester United meet FA Cup winners Chelsea at Wembley for the Charity Shield on the first Saturday of August, but their captain Roy Keane shows no charity to Gustavo Poyet, welcoming Chelsea's new signing to England by putting his studs through the Uruguayan's head with an over-the-top challenge after 17 minutes. Keane, who had been booked a week earlier for stamping his authority on French international Youri Djorkaeff at the San Siro, gets away with it this time. Later Teddy Sheringham is also lucky to stay on the pitch after leading with his elbow on Chelsea captain, Steve Clarke, just before half-time. The match ends in a draw and Chelsea win on penalties.

The following Sunday, Sheringham misses a penalty in his first Premiership

LEAGUE POSITIONS		
BLACKBURN	5	13
MAN UTD	5	13
WEST HAM	5	10
CHELSEA	4	9
ARSENAL	5	9
LEICESTER	5	8
TOTTENHAM	5	7
NEWCASTLE	2	6
CRYSTAL PALACE	5	6
BARNSLEY	5	6
LIVERPOOL	4	5
COVENTRY	5	5
BOLTON	3	3
LEEDS	5	4
SHEFF WED	5	4
DERBY	3	3
EVERTON	3	3
SOUTHAMPTON	5	3
ASTON VILLA	5	3
WIMBLEDON	4	2

match in a Manchester United shirt – against his old club Tottenham. The fans sing: "You're Spurs and you know you are," but Manchester United go straight to the top of the table after registering the only two-goal margin of victory on the first weekend of the new season.

Meanwhile, Dion Dublin kicks off with a hat-trick against Chelsea, Michael Owen scores from the spot on his Premiership debut, newcomers

Bolton and Crystal Palace open their accounts with away wins and Barnsley have a good month in their first ever season in the top flight, beating Bolton and Palace, but get a taste of things to come when Chelsea come to Yorkshire.

But at the end of the month, it is Wimbledon who prop up the table, having failed to win any of their August games, while Everton, Southampton, Villa and Derby also get off to bad starts. Derby's cause isn't helped when their first home fixture has to be abandoned after Pride Park is plunged into darkness by a floodlight failure after 56 minutes. The Rams were winning 2-1.

Back at the top, Blackburn take 13 points from their first five games as the only two clubs to have ever won the Premiership take the lead. But the month ends in mourning when the annual 4-3 thriller between Liverpool and Newcastle is postponed after the death of Diana Spencer and Dodi Fayed.

TOP GOALSCORERS	
6	Sutton
5	Bergkamp, Gallacher
4	Carbone, Vialli
3	Blake, Dublin, Ferdinand, Hartson, Petrescu, Wright

Dion Dublin collects the first hat-trick of the season on the opening day against Chelsea.

Teddy Sheringham misses from 12 yards on his return to White Hart Lane.

September

Premiership 1997

The summer ends as the next one will begin, with Arsenal shading Manchester United into first place. Leicester are within a whisker of the top spot too, as the Foxes lead the chasing pack

M anchester United begin the month by going top as David Beckham silences West Ham fans' cruel jibes about Posh Spice by curling over the cross that Paul Scholes heads in for the winner at Old Trafford. Manchester United stay top when Blackburn lose to Leeds in a sensational seven-goal thriller at Ewood Park the next day.

Arsenal maintain their challenge as Ian Wright finally breaks Cliff Bastin's record of 178 Gunner goals in 396 games. Having showed uncharacteristic nerves in front of goal all month, the 33-year-old's hat-trick against Bolton at Highbury takes him past the post. "People were saying the record was getting to me and now I can look back and say yes, it was eating into me," the England striker reflects. Wright hadn't scored since netting twice against Coventry in August, but finally reaches his tally of 180 in just 261 matches.

His England teammate Paul Ince looks the ideal replacement for Alan Shearer as his country's captain as he inspires his new club Liverpool to victory over Sheffield Wednesday.

Gustavo Poyet steals the show in Chelsea's decisive 3-0 victory over Crystal Palace, Aston Villa's Mark Draper is the star of their win at Barnsley, while Trond Soltvedt opens his account

LEAGUE POSITIONS		
ARSENAL	9	19
MAN UTD	9	18
LEICESTER	9	18
CHELSEA	8	16
BLACKBURN	9	16
LEEDS	9	13
WEST HAM	9	13
DERBY	7	12
LIVERPOOL	8	12
NEWCASTLE	6	12
CRYSTAL PALACE	9	11
COVENTRY	9	11
TOTTENHAM	9	10
ASTON VILLA	9	10
WIMBLEDON	8	9
BOLTON	8	8
EVERTON	8	8
SHEFF WED	9	6
BARNSLEY	9	6
SOUTHAMPTON	9	4

in England with Coventry's winner over struggling Southampton.

Leicester, who are preparing to meet Atletico Madrid in the UEFA Cup, have the best of Spurs at Filbert Street. The travelling support call for Gerry Francis to be replaced as manager – not for the last time. Liverpool and Villa's involvement in European competition makes the fixtures pile up; their meeting is just one of three games in six days for both clubs. Meanwhile,

Wimbledon's win at St James Park lifts them off the bottom. "We were motivated by all the things that have gone on here before," Vinnie Jones says. In the same fixture two seasons ago, club captain Jones played in goal in a 6-1 defeat.

A week later, dreadlocked teenager Danny Cadamarteri scores on his debut for Everton. There's disappointment for West Ham when John Barnes, who had just refused to join the London club following his release from Liverpool, finds himself in the Newcastle team. He answers the Hammers fans who boo him with a beautifully flighted winner from the edge of the box. But the Irons end the month on a happy note when an Eyal Berkovic winner defeats Liverpool to keep the Londoners within sight of the leaders. Meanwhile down on the South Coast, Berkovic's former club, Southampton, sink straight to the bottom with only one point to show for the entire month.

TOP GOALSCORERS	
8	Bergkamp, Sutton, Wright
6	Gallacher
5	Carbone, Hartson, Wallace
4	Baiano, Dublin, Overmars, Vialli

Vinnie Jones in his last season for the Dons before moving north of the river to QPR.

October

Premiership 1997

The League starts to settle down into what will become a familiar look as Manchester United regain the leadership. Arsenal and Blackburn are hot on their heels

Southampton start to show glimpses of improvement under new manager Dave Jones and move off the bottom of the table. The Saints are boosted by the return of Matthew Le Tissier from a broken arm sustained in a pre-season friendly. The captain directs the Saints to a convincing victory over in-form West Ham to reignite pub conversations around the country concerning his right to play for England at France '98.

Matty Elliot is one player who will be going to France with Scotland, but there is disappointment for the inspirational Leicester captain at club level. The Foxes slip up after a great start and manage to lose two games on the trot as they fall off the pace.

But the two players who steal the show on the last Premiership weekend before England's final World Cup showdown in Rome are both foreign; Patrick Berger collects his first hat-trick for Liverpool in a thriller with Chelsea, while Ian Wright says of his Dutch strike partner: "There is no question he is the best in the world," after Dennis Bergkamp is absolutely brilliant as Arsenal trounce Barnsley.

Of the latest England squad, both Gary Pallister and Teddy Sheringham give commanding performances for Manchester United, Steve McManaman

LEAGUE POSITIONS		
MAN UTD	12	25
ARSENAL	12	24
BLACKBURN	12	23
LEICESTER	12	21
CHELSEA	11	19
LIVERPOOL	11	18
DERBY	11	17
LEEDS	12	17
WIMBLEDON	12	16
NEWCASTLE	9	16
WEST HAM	12	16
CRYSTAL PALACE	12	15
ASTON VILLA	12	14
TOTTENHAM	12	13
COVENTRY	12	13
EVERTON	11	12
BOLTON	11	11
SOUTHAMPTON	12	10
SHEFF WED	12	9
BARNSLEY	12	9

and Paul Ince are magnificent against Chelsea, while their Anfield colleague Robbie Fowler returns from injury after seven weeks out of the game to stake his claim with a goal in each of his three Premiership starts.

The Derby/Wimbledon game is replayed this month, and the home team pay for the floodlight failure in August by dropping two points to the Dons. Derby, like their lights, and like their enigmatic Costa Rican striker

Paulo Wanchope, are blowing hot and cold but thay have come a long way under Jim Smith and look capable of beating anybody on their day.

But one team is beating everybody. Manchester United move up into second gear and spend the month unbeaten. They even have the gall to rub it in to Arsenal that it is the Red Devils who are the early favourites by going two better than their closest rivals in beating Barnsley 7-0.

Blackburn, with both their strikers scoring regularly, are looking a lot better under Roy Hodgson. They also take seven points from three games. Liverpool too, despite their Merseyside derby defeat, begin to climb towards the top, ending the month with a convincing victory over Derby, though the Reds' manager Roy Evans remains less popular with the fans than his counterpart at Ewood Park.

TOP GOALSCORERS	
10	Bergkamp, Sutton
9	Wright
8	Baiano
7	Carbone, Hartson
6	Gallacher
5	Berkovic, Cole, Fowler, Wallace

Hot shot Kevin Gallacher is firing home the goals for both Blackburn Rovers and Scotland.

November

Premiership 1997

Manchester United are still improving and are now averaging over two points per game. This puts some space between themselves and Chelsea, who have risen to second place

Manchester United move up into third gear, putting six past Wednesday, five past Wimbledon and four past leadership rivals Blackburn. But Rovers stay third and are still in contention when Manchester United lose a five-goal thriller at Highbury. This result will later prove to be crucial to the Championship run in, but that much is not yet apparent; the win over Manchester United gives Arsenal their only points for the month as Arsene Wenger's men slip down into fifth.

Even Liverpool's faltering challenge gets a boost at Highbury. But that much is not surprising; it is the Reds' fourth win there in six visits since the Premiership began. A well-taken goal from stand-in captain Steve McManaman earns Roy Evans' team all three points. The beleaguered boss answers the critics who had called for his head after the home defeat to Barnsley the week before by saying: "I just get on with it, I will do my best. I know if I don't then I will go the way of so many others." But his best still doesn't look good enough for Liverpool fans who have come to expect trophies every season.

Liverpool end the month outside the UEFA Cup frame and behind upstarts Leicester, who themselves need

LEAGUE POSITIONS		
MAN UTD	16	34
CHELSEA	16	31
BLACKBURN	16	30
LEEDS	16	29
ARSENAL	16	27
LEICESTER	16	26
LIVERPOOL	15	25
NEWCASTLE	13	24
DERBY	15	23
CRYSTAL PALACE	15	19
WIMBLEDON	16	19
WEST HAM	15	19
ASTON VILLA	16	18
SHEFF WED	16	18
COVENTRY	16	17
SOUTHAMPTON	16	16
TOTTENHAM	16	16
BOLTON	15	16
BARNSLEY	16	13
EVERTON	16	12

their home form to improve if they are going to maintain their early challenge.

Leeds win four out of four as George Graham's defensively orientated team start to become effective at the other end of the pitch. They have Rod Wallace playing up front, and the former midfielder has taken well to his first season in attack. But it is Chelsea who go second with the help of five goals from Gianfranco Zola, including the Sardinian's first hat-trick for the

club against Derby. Zola collects the match ball and says: "I waited for the referee in the tunnel for the ball. He could not escape. I was waiting." But Zola is also still waiting to get back into the Italy team.

Bolton's strikers' inability to score sees the club slip into the bottom three. Sheffield Wednesday put five past them as the Owls hit a vein of form to move out of the danger zone.

No-one is surprised to see Barnsley struggling but Everton are going from bad to worse on the pitch and are in turmoil off it. They lose five out of five in November to go bottom. There is further trouble for the Toffeemen when a yellow card in the home defeat against Spurs, who now have Christian Gross in charge, means that Slaven Bilic will miss December. Chairman Peter Johnson insists he will stay at Goodison Park, as does returning manager Howard Kendall.

TOP GOALSCORERS	
10	Bergkamp, Hartson, Sutton
9	Baiano, Wright
8	Cole, Wallace
7	Carbone, Dublin, Gallacher, Sheringham, Zola
6	Davies, Di Canio, Fowler, Wanchope

Barnsley players celebrate Ashley Ward's surprise winner at Anfield in November

Dean Holdsworth shields the ball from Dominic Matteo as Bolton meet Liverpool

December

Premiership 1997

In the fixture-heavy winter programme, Manchester United press their case for another title with victory over Liverpool. Blackburn and Chelsea look the only sides capable of getting past them now

The top of the table is beginning to look settled as Manchester United, with Andy Cole back to his goalscoring best, cruise into a five point lead over Blackburn and Chelsea. Man United end Liverpool's good run and then beat out-of-form Newcastle, Villa and Everton. But Cole cannot add to the 2-1 lead Sheringham gives the team just after half time at Highfield Road and they lose to two dramatic goals in the last five minutes – just to give the others a chance to catch up.

Chelsea take advantage by showing no mercy to Spurs as their rivals are brought down to earth after their end-of-November win over Everton at Goodison. Tore Andre Flo is starting to prove that he is more than a gangling target man. Chelsea then win well at Hillsborough, but two home draws keep them from going within striking distance of Manchester United.

Blackburn Rovers stay unbeaten all month but also throw away their chance to catch up on the leaders by dropping two points at home to Crystal Palace. Tim Flowers does his England hopes no good on the second goal but fellow potential international Chris Sutton caps a fine all-round performance by scoring the equaliser and sparing his keeper's blushes.

LEAGUE POSITIONS		
MAN UTD	21	46
BLACKBURN	21	41
CHELSEA	20	39
LIVERPOOL	20	37
LEEDS	21	35
ARSENAL	20	34
DERBY	21	32
WEST HAM	21	31
LEICESTER	21	28
ASTON VILLA	21	26
NEWCASTLE	20	26
WIMBLEDON	20	24
COVENTRY	21	23
CRYSTAL PALACE	21	23
SHEFF WED	21	23
SOUTHAMPTON	20	21
BOLTON	21	21
EVERTON	21	20
TOTTENHAM	21	20
BARNSLEY	21	18

Liverpool end the month on a high at St James Park, where the Magpies are still struggling to find form. They play the games in hand that everyone expects will take them up towards the top of the table but can only manage to take two points from an intensive December programme of seven games. Meanwhile, Leeds slip up and Arsenal look like also rans.

Liverpool come back into form with four successive wins after the defeat to Manchester United, but that first result of the month keeps them out of range of the top. Just behind them are Derby, while West Ham are proving pre-season doubters wrong by climbing into the frame for a UEFA Cup place. Leicester have a disastrous month in their bid to get back into that competition, taking only two points all December.

Below them, Bolton and Spurs are still hovering around the drop zone. Although Everton have a better month, their results are still not good enough to get them out of the bottom three.

Barnsley are still living down to expectations, though Ashley Ward's fifth goal in 16 games keeps the Tykes in touch with a battling win over Derby. Palace are another team on the slide and so, as the New Year begins, there are questions about all the newly-promoted sides' chances of staying the course in the Premiership.

TOP GOALSCORERS	
12	Cole, Sutton
11	Baiano, Hartson
10	Bergkamp, Gallacher, Wright
9	Fowler
8	Davies, Dublin, McManaman, Sheringham, Wallace
7	Blake, Carbone, Di Canio, Huckerby, Zola

David Unsworth made a n excellent move from
Everton to the Hammers in 1997

January

Premiership 1997

Alex Ferguson's red army has stormed the league so far, but are now only just hanging on to their lead. If the chasing pack could only start winning themselves, Manchester United might be in trouble

M anchester United are brilliant against Chelsea in the FA Cup but are beginning to stumble in the league. They start the year with a win over Spurs, but lose at the Dell for the third year running and then go down 1-0 at Old Trafford to Leicester. Blackburn Rovers miss the chance to go second at the start of the month by losing to Derby, but maintain their challenge with a 5-0 win over Villa, who, despite the return of Dwight Yorke after injury, are playing so badly they're being booed by their own fans. Things come to a head during the Blackburn game when Savo Milosevic is accused of spitting at Villa fans who chant: "You're not fit to wear the shirt!"

Arsenal make it ten games unbeaten after their win against Southampton at the Dell but then lose to Coventry, whose victory is marred by the dismissal of Paul Williams. Gordon Strachan calls Stephen Lodge "an absolute disgrace" for his refereeing of a match which also saw Patrick Vieira sent off prior to Dion Dublin's penalty.

Wednesday stay unbeaten, taking three points at Elland Road and being unlucky not to beat Wimbledon. Liverpool also hit a vein of league form after their FA Cup defeat by Coventry, despite persistent rumours that Steve

McManaman is on his way to Barcelona. Derby have both Sturridge and Wanchope on form to keep them in the frame for the UEFA Cup.

Chelsea bounce back from their FA Cup exit with an upturn in home form. The Blues end the month with a Mark Hughes-inspired win over Barnsley, who stay bottom despite beating Palace. It's Danny Wilson's turn to be upset with the refereeing now, but the sparkling form of new signings Jan Aage Fjortoft

and Ashley Ward helps to keep the Tykes optimistic.

Around them, Newcastle continue to slide, while Spurs sign Nicola Berti and Jürgen Klinsmann, but fail to get Andy Hinchcliffe and Patrick Blondeau to shore up their leaky defence. West Ham fans, who had sung "Down with the Spurs" to Barnsley fans the month before, now see Klinsmann earn the points at Upton Park.

Bolton take only one point all month, but that's still one more than Palace. Meanwhile, Everton, now with Madar spurring Barmby and Ferguson into form, take nine from nine, including their second away win in a month. They had previously gone nearly a year without a result away from Goodison. Now their troubles seem finally to be over as they edge their way back up the league. Or do they?

LEAGUE POSITIONS		
MAN UTD	24	49
CHELSEA	24	45
BLACKBURN	24	45
LIVERPOOL	24	45
ARSENAL	23	41
DERBY	24	39
LEEDS	24	38
WEST HAM	24	35
LEICESTER	24	33
SHEFF WED	24	30
NEWCASTLE	23	29
SOUTHAMPTON	24	28
COVENTRY	24	27
EVERTON	24	27
ASTON VILLA	23	27
WIMBLEDON	23	26
CRYSTAL PALACE	24	23
TOTTENHAM	24	23
BOLTON	24	22
BARNSLEY	24	21

TOP GOALSCORERS	
13	Gallacher, Sutton
12	Bergkamp, Cole, Hartson
11	Baiano, Dublin
10	Wright
9	Fowler, Huckerby, Sturridge, Wallace
8	Blake, Di Canio, Hasselbaink, McManaman, Sheringham, Wanchope

Sol Campbell keeps an eye on Dean Sturridge but Derby take the points at Pride Park

Arsenal's wide midfield partnership of Parlour and Overmars celebrates another goal

February

Premiership 1997

Finally Manchester United start to put distance between themselves and the rest of the field, while at the bottom Crystal Palace start to tumble down, but there's still a long way to go

When Manchester United beat Chelsea for the second time in just over a month, this time at Stamford Bridge in the league, the Red Devils look a different class from the chasing pack. Forty years on from Münich, and Man United are back on top of the world. Comparisons are inevitably made between the team of 1958 and the team of 1998, but the true difference between the leaders and the rest of the Premiership this season is that while Manchester United consistently get results, none of their challengers can string two wins together.

Vanquished Chelsea lose both their other games this month and so Blackburn go second despite two 3-0 defeats. Liverpool's improvement now looks a false dawn as they fail to win any of their four matches, and that means that Arsenal's two wins lift the Gunners into third. But they are still 12 points behind Man United with only 13 matches to go, and although their FA Cup run means they have three games in hand on the leaders, surely the gap is too great now.

Derby and Leeds aren't taking advantage of the opportunity to catch up on the UEFA Cup placed teams, but Coventry win four on the spin with Dion Dublin playing the captain's part.

LEAGUE POSITIONS		
MAN UTD	28	59
BLACKBURN	27	48
ARSENAL	25	47
LIVERPOOL	28	47
CHELSEA	27	45
DERBY	28	45
LEICESTER	28	40
LEEDS	27	39
WEST HAM	26	39
COVENTRY	28	39
SOUTHAMPTON	28	37
NEWCASTLE	27	34
SHEFF WED	28	34
ASTON VILLA	28	33
WIMBLEDON	26	32
EVERTON	28	30
TOTTENHAM	28	30
BARNSLEY	27	25
BOLTON	27	24
CRYSTAL PALACE	27	23

Disbelieving Coventry fans even see their team move onto the first page of Teletext but their eyes are not yet set on Europe. Rather, the talk is of being just two wins from safety, such is the extent to which the club is used to their annual relegation battle.

Although fellow perennial relegation candidates Southampton lose to the Sky Blues at the Dell, the Saints also beat three other teams above them in the league this month. They get excellent results at Anfield and Elland Road to put them right behind Coventry. West Ham also show away form to match their performances at Upton Park. Leicester are getting results too, but defeat at Blackburn keeps the Foxes just out of touch with the top six.

Meanwhile Newcastle and Aston Villa are not living up to pre-season expectations. Rather than chasing for Europe, they are both looking over their shoulders at the places Coventry and Southampton usually occupy. But though Wednesday and Wimbledon would also have hoped to be better placed by now, it's Everton and Spurs who are at the bottom. It's lucky for them that Bolton and Palace can't win all month, though Barnsley beat Wimbledon and earn a point against Everton to keep hope alive.

TOP GOALSCORERS	
16	Sutton
14	Dublin
13	Cole, Gallacher, Owen
12	Bergkamp, Hartson
11	Baiano
10	Di Canio, Huckerby, Wallace Wanchope, Wright
9	Blake, Davies, Ferguson, Fowler, Sturridge

Graeme Le Saux back in a Chelsea shirt
after four years at Blackburn Rovers

March

Premiership 1997

Spring fever, as Arsenal clinch the points from their exciting match against Manchester United and turn the tables on the Champions. Suddenly the Premiership is wide open again...

Even when Manchester United take only one point from their two away games at the start of the month, they are still everyone's favourites. But when they lose the big one at home to Arsenal, it all changes. Arsenal haven't been called boring all season, but they are in 1-0 mode now and that result at Old Trafford means that the destiny of the championship is in the Gunners' hands for the first time. Defeat there would have left them still nine points behind the leaders with two games in hand. Now they are just three points off the top. If Arsenal keep winning, and there's little evidence to say they won't, they will win the league, whatever Man United manage during the remainder of the campaign.

Behind these two, Liverpool are getting the better of some high-scoring matches but it looks too little too late. The Reds go above Blackburn and Chelsea but all these three teams can hope for now is a UEFA Cup place. Barring an incredible loss of form by Manchester United and Arsenal, the race for the Premiership has now come down to these two teams.

West Ham hold both contenders at Upton Park and also beat Leeds there on a fateful night for the travelling party as their plane faults on take-off

from Stansted airport. Both are now the best placed teams for the last automatic UEFA Cup spot after Derby lose three in a row, including an emphatic five-goal home drubbing at the hands of a rejuvenated Leeds.

Coventry and Southampton both still have an outside hope of Europe and are safe from relegation now. Villa are coming good at last too, though the home defeat by Barnsley tells its own sorry story of a defence that was

arguably the best in the country last year, but which has failed to show any consistency in the present campaign.

Leicester lose to Wednesday, the match is one of the first meaningless mid-table clashes of the final phases of this season. Neither side now looks capable of finishing in the top six.

Towards the other end, Wimbledon are still not out of the woods, while Newcastle are continuing to slide despite the return of Alan Shearer. Tottenham and Everton are now in serious trouble. An average of a-point-a-game is relegation form, especially when the two teams below you are doing slightly better. Bolton and Barnsley are still battling, though Palace look doomed. A great result at St James Park is all they manage for the month. They can't win at home, and now look like going straight back down because of it

LEAGUE POSITIONS		
MAN UTD	32	63
ARSENAL	30	60
LIVERPOOL	31	54
BLACKBURN	30	51
CHELSEA	30	48
LEEDS	31	48
WEST HAM	30	47
DERBY	30	45
COVENTRY	30	43
SOUTHAMPTON	31	43
ASTON VILLA	32	42
LEICESTER	30	40
SHEFF WED	31	37
WIMBLEDON	30	36
NEWCASTLE	31	36
TOTTENHAM	31	34
EVERTON	31	33
BARNSLEY	31	31
BOLTON	31	30
CRYSTAL PALACE	31	26

TOP GOALSCORERS	
16	Sutton
14	Dublin, Gallacher, Owen
13	Bergkamp, Cole, Hartson
11	Baiano, Di Canio, Huckerby, McManaman
10	Blake, Hasselbaink, Wallace, Wanchope, Wright

Andy Booth gets the better of Tony Adams at Highbury, but it's Dennis Bergkamp who gets the winner for the Champions elect

Crystal Palace's latest signing Thomas Brolin takes some advice from Attilio Lombardo

April

Though it seemed impossible at Christmas, it's all over before the fat lady sings this year as Arsenal rack up a record Premiership winning streak that leaves even Manchester United for dead

Arsenal continue to clock up the wins and so even when Manchester United win at a stroll at Selhurst Park against now relegated Crystal Palace, Alex Ferguson admits that the Gunners have overtaken his team as favourites to win the Premiership. It's not over Ferguson is philosophical as he faces the prospect of defeat. He knows that even if Arsenal do keep on getting results, Manchester United cannot now fail to finish second; the draw against Liverpool ensured that. And second place is good enough to qualify for the Champions League next season, which is the trophy Ferguson is really after. It is still a bitter disappointment for Manchester United fans all around the world that their team failed to sustain their early season form to wrap up the title by Easter.

Liverpool look safe and satisfied in third place, while Chelsea also know by the end of the month that they will take a UEFA Cup place. Not that they need it.

They have already qualified for the competition on the basis of their Coca-Cola Cup success. They also have the Cup Winners' Cup final to look forward to in May, and with it the prospect of joining this year's FA Cup finalists Newcastle in that tournament next

season, providing they can can overcome VfB Stuttgart.

Of the rest of last season's European representatives, Leicester are still in with a shout, especially if Chelsea do beat Stuttgart to open up another UEFA Cup place in the league. Villa too are still improving after a poor season to sneak a place. But these teams will have to wait until the very end to know their fate. But Leeds earn a string of results that ensures they end

April almost certain to be playing in Europe next year, while Blackburn look good for the fourth automatic UEFA Cup place. Outsiders West Ham and Derby will probably have to look forward to a renewed challenge in August.

Last year's runners up Newcastle are still floundering in the second half of the table, but survival has been assured, albeit below Coventry and Southampton, who are both quite safe.

With the exception of Wednesday, the rest are still in deep trouble. Although it seems increasingly likely that it will be the three promoted teams who go straight back down, Spurs and Wimbledon have a big six-pointer coming up with Premiership survival as the prize.

And Everton are deep in the mire with with goalkeeper Thomas Myhre still too often to be found deep in his own net retrieving the ball.

LEAGUE POSITIONS

ARSENAL	37	78
MAN UTD	37	74
LIVERPOOL	37	65
CHELSEA	37	60
LEEDS	37	58
BLACKBURN	37	55
ASTON VILLA	37	54
LEICESTER	37	53
WEST HAM	37	53
DERBY	37	52
COVENTRY	37	51
SOUTHAMPTON	37	47
NEWCASTLE	37	44
SHEFF WED	37	44
TOTTENHAM	37	43
WIMBLEDON	37	43
BOLTON	37	40
EVERTON	37	39
BARNSLEY	37	35
CRYSTAL PALACE	37	30

TOP GOALSCORERS

17	Sutton
16	Bergkamp, Dublin, Gallacher, Hasselbaink, Owen
15	Cole, Hartson
14	Huckerby
12	Baiano, Di Canio
11	Blake, Ferguson, McManaman, Ostenstad, Wanchope

Dennis Irwin and Danny Murphy tussle for the ball during the 1-1 draw at Old Trafford

Theo Zagorakis and Michele Padovano in action at Selhurst Park before both are substituted in Leicester's 3-0 win

GUNNERS GLORY

Premiership 1997

Remember 1989 and that Michael Thomas goal at Anfield that won the League on the last day of the season? That couldn't have been any closer. Better to win with two games left before the Cup Final...

After ten straight wins and an unbeaten run that stretched back 18 games, Arsenal clinched the title with the 4-0 defeat of Everton on the first weekend in May.

It was the Gunners' first title since 1991 and the first time a non-British manager had won the English League.

"It is my best achievement in football" Arsène Wenger said after the game. He also admits for the first time that he hadn't believed at the start of the season that a team with so many new players could win the Premiership, and also confessing that when his side had dropped 13 points off the pace in the New Year, he again believed the race to be over, at least as far as Arsenal were concerned.

Now in retrospect, it seems obvious that a team that lost four times in the league all season before taking the title should have the advantage over one

that lost seven, but Manchester United were still hot favourites right up until the two sides met in March, the game Wenger described as "the turning point." But it still required a Premiership-record run from the Gunners after that match to oust their rivals from the top spot.

Arsenal's consistency in the run-in can in part be attributed to the fact that the manager was able to put out pretty much the same side throughout the crucial Easter period.

Protecting England's best defence this spring was the increasingly excellent midfield quartet of Parlour, Vieira, Petit and Overmars. On the right flank, Ray Parlour may still not have the technique that Overmars displays on the left, but he has improved enough this season to get into the England squad, while the central partnership of Vieira and Petit must be

giving Aime Jacquet headaches as he selects his midfield for the World Cup from a vast army of world class players.

Talking of world class, the Arsenal front line was without its prime star Dennis Bergkamp for most of the last stretch. His enforced absence with hamstring trouble still didn't give Ian Wright a place in the starting line up. But Wrighty, who had not started a game since being injured in January, would be given his run out on the final day of glory. Although it was left to Tony Adams to bury the fourth goal with the aplomb Wright has so often shown in the past.

The captain's crowning goal was the perfect end to a perfect season for the Gunners and for many, many neutrals around the world who had soaked up the historic run-in. But, from a team of giants, who was Wenger's player of the season? "Team spirit," he smiled.

THE FORM OF CHAMPIONS The ten wins that took the Premiership title to Highbury

11/3/98	Wimbledon	0	**Arsenal**	1		13/4/98	Blackburn	1	**Arsenal**	4
14/3/98	Man U	0	**Arsenal**	1		18/4/98	**Arsenal**	5	Wimbledon	0
28/3/98	**Arsenal**	1	Sheff Wed	0		25/4/98	Barnsley	0	**Arsenal**	2
31/3/98	Bolton	0	**Arsenal**	1		29/4/98	**Arsenal**	1	Derby	0
11/4/98	**Arsenal**	3	Newcastle	1		2/5/98	**Arsenal**	4	Everton	0

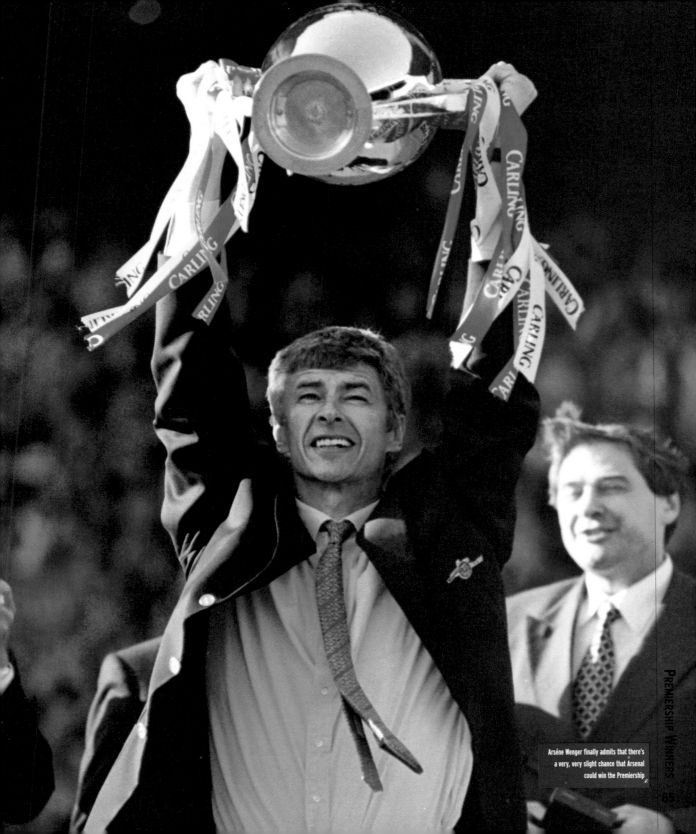

Arséne Wenger finally admits that there's a very, very slight chance that Arsenal could win the Premiership

Tony Adam's: goalscorer supreme. This time it's a net-buster against Southampton at Highbury

Boa Morte powers through a challenge from Southampton's Kevin Richardson

Ian Wright stand-in Luis Boa Morte
beats Palace's Valerien Ismael for pace

Patrick Viera shows why Arsenal's midfield was the most
feared in the country. John Moncur disagrees...

PREMERSHIP WINNERS

87

"1-0 to the Arsenal!", Overmars (left) and Winterburn ensure a home win against Sheffield Wednesday

Ray Parlour forces hapless West Ham midfielder John Moncur into some "direct" defensive tactics

A changed man? Ray Parlour's form in 1997-98 was a revelation to Arsenal fans and to Glen Hoddle

Scenes of celebration on Arsenal's travels became more and more commonplace in 1998

Tony Adams recovers from his screamer against Everton, only to discover a huge trophy in his hands

Out-and-out hero and unsung hero. Nigel Winterburn explains to a friend of his that winning really is everything

"Too old?"... yeah right. Adams and Wrighty display all the evidence anyone needs that experience really does count

Marc Overmars came through a fallow period to emerge as the stylist and speed-meister Wenger demanded

Now who's Butthead's mate? So-called Beavis look-a-like, Denis Bergkamp looks at yet another trophy

The final games
10th May 1998

With the Championship already decided, the interest on the final day of the season centred around the relegation battle between Everton and Bolton

There were UEFA Cup places to be decided, and a million permutations to be worked out, with all the clubs as far down the Premiership as Coventry still in with a mathematical chance of qualifying for Europe, but the big story on the final day of the season concerned the battle to avoid the third relegation place.

Would Bolton Wanderers, who had been relegated the last time they played in the Premiership, go straight back down again, or would Everton, who have been in the top flight of English football for longer than any other club, finally take the drop that their performances this season have probably deserved?

Sitting just one point above their rivals in the relative safety of 17th place, Bolton went into the final game at Stamford Bridge knowing that three points there would ensure their survival, whatever Everton managed at home to Coventry. The Toffeemen knew that they needed to take more points from their last game than Bolton did. A draw would do if Bolton lost, as their goal difference was superior, but 10-0 wouldn't be enough if the Trotters managed to get a result.

Everton were given an early boost when Gareth Farrelly scored from the

THE MATCHES	WHAT'S AT STAKE
Aston Villa v Arsenal	UEFA cup place for Aston Villa
Barnsley v Manchester United	Nothing at stake
Blackburn v Newcastle	UEFA cup place for Blackburn
Chelsea v Bolton	Relegation for Bolton
Crystal Palace v Sheffield Wednesday	Nothing at stake
Derby v Liverpool	UEFA cup place for Derby
Everton v Coventry	Relegation for Everton UEFA cup place for Coventry
Leeds v Wimbledon	Nothing at stake
Tottenham v Southampton	Nothing at stake
West Ham v Leicester	UEFA cup place for West Ham UEFA cup place for Leicester

edge of the area in the first half, but Gordon Strachan was still urging his players on as if their own survival depended upon it, and so even when the news came in that Chelsea had scored Everton still had to maintain their lead. The Toffeemen looked to have it sealed up when they were awarded a dubious penalty late in the match after substitute Danny Cadamarteri was up-ended in the box. However Nicky Barmby hit his shot too

high and too centrally to give Hedman any trouble in saving it. Then Dion Dublin rose above the Everton defence to head home his 18th of the season and suddenly the Everton faithful, who had been singing ever since Farrelly's goal, were subdued again. Chelsea had gone 2-0 up over Bolton, but a late Coventry winner would still have been enough to send Kendall's men down.

Meanwhile down at Stamford Bridge, the whole ground was egging Bolton on to score. Even the Chelsea fans were booing their own players as they, like most of the country, were supporting the underdogs in this final relegation battle. But after Jody Morris' goal, Bolton now needed to score twice to stay up, and this they couldn't do.

And so Everton held on, albeit uncomfortably, for the draw that kept them up, but rather than singing the team's praises after the final whistle went, Goodison Park reverberated to the chant of: "We want Johnson out."

Elsewhere the teams that had found themselves a place in Europe next season were Arsenal, Manchester United (Champions' League), Liverpool, Leeds, Blackburn (UEFA Cup), Newcastle (Cup Winners' Cup), plus Aston Villa into the UEFA Cup, if Chelsea win the Cup Winners' Cup this season.

Sad Bolton: but a round of hands for their loyal fans as they face life in Division One again

It may all be done as far as Arsenal is concerned, but Joachim still wants to win

Trevor Sinclair and Rio Ferdinand celebrate West Ham's third goal against Leicester

The statistics
Premiership 1997-98

The full record of the Premiership table; all the games and all the goals. Plus the final top goalscorer charts as well as the statistics for this season's referees

	P	HOME RECORD					AWAY RECORD					Pts	GD
		W	D	L	F	A	W	D	L	F	A		
Arsenal	38	15	2	2	43	10	8	7	4	25	23	**78**	35
Man Utd	38	13	4	2	42	9	10	4	5	31	17	**77**	47
Liverpool	38	13	2	4	42	16	5	9	5	26	26	**65**	26
Chelsea	38	13	2	4	37	14	7	1	11	34	29	**63**	28
Leeds	38	9	5	5	31	21	8	3	8	26	25	**59**	11
Blackburn	38	11	4	4	40	26	5	6	8	17	26	**58**	5
Aston Villa	38	9	3	7	26	24	8	3	8	23	24	**57**	1
West Ham	38	13	4	2	40	18	3	4	12	16	39	**56**	-1
Derby	38	12	3	4	33	18	4	4	11	19	31	**55**	3
Leicester	38	6	10	3	21	15	7	4	8	30	26	**53**	10
Coventry	38	8	9	2	26	17	4	7	8	20	27	**52**	2
Southampton	38	10	1	8	28	23	4	5	10	22	32	**48**	-5
Newcastle	38	8	5	6	22	20	3	6	10	13	24	**44**	-9
Tottenham	38	7	8	4	23	22	4	3	12	21	34	**44**	-12
Wimbledon	38	5	6	8	18	25	5	8	6	16	21	**44**	-12
Sheff Wed	38	9	5	5	30	26	3	3	13	22	41	**44**	-15
Everton	38	7	5	7	25	27	2	8	9	16	29	**40**	-15
Bolton	38	7	8	4	25	22	2	5	12	16	39	**40**	-20
Barnsley	38	7	4	8	25	35	3	1	15	12	47	**35**	-45
Crystal Palace	38	2	5	12	15	39	6	4	9	22	32	**33**	-36

FINAL GOALSCORERS

18 Dublin, Owen, Sutton
16 Bergkamp, Cole, Gallacher, Hasselbaink
15 Hartson
14 Huckerby
12 Baiano, Blake, Di Canio, Wanchope

REFEREE	GAMES				REFEREE	GAMES				REFEREE	GAMES		
Alcock	20	59	1		Durkin	19	61	4		Rennie	19	79	5
Ashby	19	56	2		Elleray	18	64	5		Riley	26	67	4
Barber	22	90	7		Gallagher	19	50	3		Wilkie	22	73	2
Barry	20	68	2		Jones	21	57	2		Willard	21	92	8
Bodenham	21	65	1		Lodge	21	54	3		Winter	20	79	2
Burge	19	48	4		Poll	21	83	10					
Dunn	16	52	2		Reed	19	84	2					